GWYN

THE LIFE OF AN UNSUNG SOLDIER

Stuart Morgan

Copyright © 2024 Stuart Morgan

All rights reserved.

ISBN: 9798879730241

DEDICATION

To the memory of my grandfather, and those he left behind.

Also, to my children, Ella Rose & Freddie Gwyn Morgan.

CONTENTS

	Introduction	i
1	A Welsh Beginning	1
2	The Looming Threat	18
3	Anti-Aircraft Defence	29
4	The Northeast	40
5	The Move to Middlesbrough	58
6	Call to Duty on The Continent	77
7	Dunkirk Evacuation	90
8	A Hero's Return	118
9	Transfer to Kent	131
10	The Ormonde	148
11	Arriving In North Africa	164
12	Progress In Northern Africa	174
13	The Italian Job	188
14	Back In Training	198
15	The Advance on Forli	209
16	Greece	226
17	Crete	244
18	Back To Blighty	254

Introduction

On the 14th of December 1993, my grandfather, Gwyn Morgan, passed away from a heart attack at his home in Spring Gardens, Letterston, Pembrokeshire. He left behind his wife Mary Ann, his Children, Gwyneth, Shirley, Gareth and Perry, and his grandchildren, Mickey, Sandra, Christopher, Simon, Laura, Siwan, Cerys, Kenny and me, Stuart.

People say you don't miss what you've never had, and I suppose in some way that's true. Born in October 1992, I was only 1 when he passed away, so I have no recollection of him. I was in my late teens before I first recall seeing a photograph of him. Until then, he was little more than a name to me. In fact, I wasn't 100% sure of his name. I only remember him being referred to as 'Pop'. So, I can't say I ever had the opportunity to miss him as such, but what I have always felt is curiosity. Hearing my aunts, uncles, parents, and cousins speak about him always left me with a sense that I was missing out on something but I was unable to put my finger on exactly what that was.

Growing up, I felt the void of his loss without realising it. It was only as I grew older that I felt the need to ask questions about his life. I had close relationships with all my other grandparents, and although it was no fault of my own, a part of me felt guilt for not being able to have a relationship with him.

As I entered my late twenties and had children of my own, my desire to understand my roots and learn more about my ancestors grew. Not only for myself but for my children. In this day and age, with social media and the technology we have access to, memories of our lives will always be accessible through posts and photographs shared on Facebook, Instagram and almost every social media platform you could imagine. Meaning in a hundred years, it's likely that our grandchildren, great-grandchildren, or even great-great-grandchildren will remember us with ease. If they wondered, 'How did my great-grandmother celebrate her 40th birthday?' It would not take too much detective work to find the photographs of a boozy weekend in Cardiff. But if you were to ask that question to yourself, what was your great-grandmother up to on her 40th birthday? It's safe to say there is no way of knowing.

It's for that reason that I feel the need to continue the memory of those relatives who came before us. Researching my ancestry quickly gathered momentum and soon I was able to trace ancestors back generations. From the Morgans who sailed to America in the 1800's to start a new life, to those who farmed the lands of Pembrokeshire 200 years ago. Although I found this all very interesting, it was a struggle to feel any connection to these characters and stories that spanned decades. It eventually dawned on me that I knew almost as much about my 5 X great-grandfather as I did about my actual grandfather, and that just didn't sit right with me.

As a child, there were always stories mentioned of my grandfather's time serving his country during the Second World War. These stories always stuck in my mind, not because of the interesting details that enthralled me, but because of the vague nature of them. I always wanted to know more, but soon discovered that nobody had any real details to share. His refusal to speak about anything related to the war meant there were no great war stories passed down through the generations.

My research into ancient ancestors took a backseat as the number of unanswered questions I had about my grandfather stacked up. Each one chipped away at me until I decided I had to get some answers. I began by requesting birth and death certificates from the general registry office, and from there I was able to apply to the MoD for his service record. Months went by with no response, but eventually, I had a reply informing me that they were unable to find any trace of him.

Frustratingly, I continued to dig into anything I could find until I heard, through members of the family, that there was always some confusion regarding his date of birth. Both his birth and death certificates state his date of birth as the 15th of October 1918, but family members remember his birthday as the 14th. Armed with this new information, plus a copy of some fragile old documents my Aunt Shirley had dug out, I reapplied to the MoD and again, waited months for a reply.

Eventually, I did get the much-anticipated reply, telling me they had found his record. However, my joy was short-lived as they went on to inform me that although they had the reference number for the document, it had been sent to the National Archives as part of a data preservation scheme. This meant more applications and even more time spent waiting. Then again, more bad news. The document was sealed as it was less than a hundred years old, and I had to submit a freedom of information request to access it. This request was the slowest yet and dragged on for almost 18 months until I finally received what I wanted.

Naively, part of me expected a long list of places he was sent and things he was ordered to do. However, what I received was 28 pages of rushed scribbles from commanding officers as he was posted to various units and some quickly taken medical records from his enlistment. The records were mostly written in illegible numbers and abbreviations, with the occasional place name. Deciphering it took weeks, but what I ended up with was a list of regiments and batteries that he was posted to and the dates on which he was posted.

My next challenge was working out exactly what the specific batteries, of up to roughly 200 men, did. There are various forums and websites online that claim certain batteries served at certain places and did certain things, but some seem to contradict each other. So, I soon realised the only way of knowing any of this information for sure was to read the war diaries myself. Throughout the war, each regiment kept records of every movement and order they gave and received, often as thoroughly as on an hourly basis. These are all kept by the national archives and can be requested once you have found the catalogue number you require, which is easier said than done. But I slowly collected these war diaries and went through every line methodically. I toiled through thousands of pages filled with information, noting each movement, order, and conflict they encountered. This took hours upon hours and left me with several notebooks filled cover to cover with my scribbles.

I now had a pretty good understanding of his time in the army but the information I did have was largely facts and figures. Also, the information had come from commanding officers who had produced these reports and submitted them to their superiors. So, I'm sure some of these may have been slightly biased in favour of the officer who wrote them.

So, with that in mind, I wanted to find out more about these events from the men who were there, rather than the men who had sent them. This meant more digging and research. Luckily, there are endless resources out there with accounts by veterans, or their descendants that have access to their diaries or journals. There are websites dedicated to these stories, as well as thousands of books. Sifting through these to find men who served either in the same unit as my grandfather, or in similar units that were posted to the same places around the same time, proved time-consuming, but enjoyable.

Eventually, I was left with thousands of pages of information. My phone is filled with random screenshots that I 'may need,' my home is filled with folders stuffed with documents and books brimming with notes. I have files on my computer with thousands of pages of war diaries and first-hand accounts that I have either saved from the internet or scanned from various books. Using the official reports I had, along with the men who were there's interpretation of the events within the reports, I had put together a complete picture of my grandfather's time at war.

With a head and folders filled with these stories, I feel a responsibility to share them with others. In my opinion, his children, my father, aunts, and uncle, deserve to understand the sacrifices their father made, not only for them but for their country. Although they must respect his decision to suffer these memories in silence, I think it's important for them to have the opportunity to understand why he made that decision. Also, it's the responsibility of us, his grandchildren to ensure his heroics are remembered and passed on to our children and in turn theirs.

The time and effort it would take to pass the vast amount of information I have gathered down through the generations would be near impossible. That is how I decided to write this book. Although it took a lot of time, effort and money to research and put together, the thought that one day, my children could pass on the memory of my grandfather to their children makes me immensely proud. And that alone makes it worthwhile.

CHAPTER ONE

A Welsh Beginning

In 1918, amidst the global turmoil of World War I, the small village of Letterston in Pembrokeshire, Wales, remained a tranquil haven. The Morgan family home, a quaint stone cottage nestled among rolling hills and lush meadows, stood as a bastion of rural serenity. This was the world young Gwyn Morgan knew as a child – a world far removed from the upheaval of global conflicts, where life ebbed and flowed with the rhythms of nature and the enduring customs of Welsh village life.

The village itself was a picturesque shade of

cobblestone streets and thatched cottages, embodying the quintessential charm of rural Wales. Life here revolved around the community, with generations of families intertwined in a rich tapestry of shared history and mutual support. The weekly market in the village square was an explosion of activity and colour, drawing villagers into a bustling hub of trade and conversation, reinforcing the strong communal bonds that were the cornerstone of life in Letterston.

Gwyn's father, David Henry Morgan, was a man of stoic integrity, respected in the village for his hard work and dedication to his family. His mother, Sophia Jane Morgan, was the heart of the Morgan household, her warmth and kindness radiating throughout their home and into the community. In this nurturing environment, the youngest of 4 children, Gwyn grew up surrounded by love and the close-knit bonds of village life, foundations that would shape his character and worldview.

The sprawling Welsh countryside was both a playground and a classroom for young Gwyn. His days were spent exploring the verdant fields, dense forests, and meandering streams, each adventure a lesson in the subtle nuances of the natural world. These experiences were integral to understanding life in this rural setting, teaching Gwyn about the rhythms of nature, the importance of community, and the resilience required to thrive in the Welsh countryside.

However, life in Letterston was not devoid of challenges. The community faced the everyday realities of rural living – the relentless demands of farming, the instability of weather, and the necessity for mutual aid during difficult times. These challenges were met with a shared resilience, instilling in Gwyn a deep-seated belief in hard work, communal support, and the enduring strength of the human spirit.

Gwyn's early years were marked by both joy and hardship. The loss of his mother in 1922, when he was just 4, brought a profound sense of grief and loss. Yet, the strength of his family and the support of the wider community helped him navigate this tragedy, imparting lessons about the complexities of life, the fragility of happiness, and the enduring nature of love and togetherness.

The tranquillity of Gwyn's childhood stood in stark contrast to the distant echoes of change. The end of World War I had brought a fragile peace, but the undercurrents of future conflicts were already brewing. These distant rumblings of a changing world had yet to directly impact the serene life of Letterston, but they foreshadowed a shift that would inevitably influence Gwyn's journey.

Gwyn's formative years in Letterston laid a strong foundation for the person he would become. Imbued with a sense of community, resilience, and a profound connection to the natural world, these early experiences prepared him for the challenges and changes that lay ahead. As the world outside the village began to stir once more, Gwyn's life, rooted in the traditions and values of rural Wales, was set to intersect with the broader narrative of a world on the brink of transformation.

Family Ties and Early Loss

In the heart of Letterston, the Morgan household was a hub of love and laughter, a sanctuary where Gwyn's early years unfolded with the gentle rhythms of family life. David and Sophia, Gwyn's parents, had created a home brimming with warmth and stability. Their union, a cornerstone of the family's happiness, was celebrated in the community, known for its strength and devotion.

The Morgan family was not large by the standards

of rural Wales, but it was lively and full of love. Gwyn, the youngest, was doted on by his siblings – Hugh, Owen, and Margaret. The children's laughter often filled the home, a testament to the joyous and nurturing environment their parents had cultivated. These early years were a tapestry of familial moments – shared meals, evening stories by the hearth, and Sunday church services where the family joined together in harmonious unity.

Sophia, a woman of grace and kindness, was the heart of the Morgan home. Her gentle presence and nurturing touch were the pillars upon which the family's daily life rested. She instilled in her children a sense of compassion and empathy, lessons taught not through words but through her daily actions and the love she poured into every aspect of their home lives.

David, a man of few words, communicated his love through actions rather than expressions. His days were spent toiling on the family land, ensuring the sustenance and security of his family. In the evenings, he would often gather the children, sharing stories of Welsh folklore and tales of their ancestors, instilling in them a deep sense of pride in their heritage and a connection to the land that sustained them.

The tranquillity of this idyllic family life, however, was abruptly shattered in 1922. Sophia's passing during childbirth was a profound shock to the family, sending ripples of grief through the Morgan household and the wider community. Her absence left a void that was deeply felt, particularly by young Gwyn, who at 4 years old struggled to comprehend the magnitude of the loss.

The aftermath of Sophia's death saw the Morgan family grappling with their new reality. David, though stoic in his grief, was a changed man, his sorrow a silent presence in the home. The children, each dealing with their loss in different ways, found solace in each other and the collective memories of their mother. Gwyn, due to his tender age, was the most affected, his mother's absence a puzzle that his young mind could not yet piece together. Despite the absence of their mother, David maintained a connection with his children, but the family dynamic had undeniably shifted.

In the wake of the tragedy, the decision was made to send Gwyn to live with his aunt Martha, Sophia's sister, and her husband, Lewis. This transition, while challenging, brought Gwyn into a new familial circle. Martha, who bore a striking resemblance to Sophia both in appearance and temperament, enveloped Gwyn in the same kind of nurturing love he had known with his mother. Lewis, a kind-hearted and jovial man, took to Gwyn as if he were his own son, integrating him into their family.

Gwyn's move to his aunt and uncle's home marked the beginning of a new chapter in his life. Though the loss of his mother was an ever-present shadow, the love and stability provided by Martha and Lewis offered a semblance of the warmth and security he had known. In this new household, Gwyn found a second family, where he was raised not only as a nephew but also as a beloved son and brother, all while maintaining a connection with his father and siblings in the village.

Life with Aunt Martha

Gwyn's arrival at Aunt Martha and Uncle Lewis' home, nestled on the outskirts of Letterston, marked a turning point in his young life. Aunt Martha's house, named "Min-Yr-Afon," was a charming cottage surrounded by sprawling fields and a small orchard, a setting that offered both comfort and a sense of adventure to the young boy. Martha and Lewis, who went on to have three boys of their own — Glyn, Vincent, and Keith —

opened their hearts and home to Gwyn, weaving him seamlessly into the fabric of their family.

Aunt Martha, with her gentle demeanour and nurturing spirit, bore a resemblance to Sophia in the warmth she radiated. She stepped into the role of a mother figure for Gwyn, providing the love and care he so keenly missed. Her ability to blend kindness with discipline created a balanced and nurturing environment. She often spent her evenings knitting by the fireplace, a constant presence in the living room, ready with a comforting word or a listening ear for the children's daily adventures and concerns.

Uncle Lewis, a cheerful man, brought a different energy to the household. He worked at a local farm and often involved the boys in various chores, teaching them the value of hard work and the satisfaction of a job well done. Lewis had a knack for storytelling, and his tales of Welsh legends and folklore captivated Gwyn and his cousins, often becoming the highlight of their evenings. Under his guidance, Gwyn learned not only about the importance of diligence but also about the rich tapestry of Welsh history and culture.

The bond between Gwyn and his cousins grew strong, with the boys treating each other more like brothers than cousins. Glyn, the eldest, was born in the same year that Gwyn moved in. Vincent and Keith, with their boundless energy and mischievous streak, often led the group into various adventures. Together, they explored the countryside, built forts in the woods, and played games in the fields, their laughter and shouts a constant echo around Min-Yr-Afon.

Life with Aunt Martha and Uncle Lewis also brought new routines and traditions. Sundays were special, with the family attending the local church, followed by a hearty lunch prepared by Martha. These moments were more than religious observances; they were opportunities for the family to bond, reflect, and give thanks. The sense of community at these gatherings provided Gwyn with a feeling of belonging and reinforced the values of faith, family, and fellowship.

Seasonal activities added to the richness of Gwyn's life at Min-Yr-Afon. Autumn apple picking in the orchard, winter evenings spent around the fire sharing stories and hot cocoa, spring planting in the vegetable garden, and summer days filled with outdoor play and exploration – these experiences ingrained in Gwyn a deep appreciation for the rhythms of nature and the simple joys of country life.

Despite the happiness and stability Martha and Lewis provided, the absence of Gwyn's mother remained a subtle undercurrent in his life. Martha, sensitive to Gwyn's unspoken feelings, often found gentle ways to honour the memory of Sophia in their household. She kept the connection alive, ensuring that Gwyn's Mother was more than just a memory, and an integral part of his identity and history.

As Gwyn grew older under Martha and Lewis's care, he developed a resilience and adaptability that would serve him well in the years to come. Their home was not just a shelter from the loss he had experienced; it was a nurturing ground where his character was moulded, his sense of self was strengthened, and his connection to his family's past was maintained. In this loving environment, Gwyn learned the values of family, the importance of belonging, and the strength that comes from knowing one's roots.

Gwyn's Father, David, continued in his grief for Sophia throughout his life, but as the resilient character he was, he refused to allow such a tragedy to shape his life. 2 years after the loss of his beloved wife, David was remarried to Martha Nicholas, who was a positive and lively woman. Martha, sensitive to the family's loss, became an important part of the family. She never tried to replace Sophia, but her maternal nature gave the children a natural figure to love and appreciate. David and Martha went on to have two children of their own, Vivian and Ada. The whole family became a blend of biological parentage, but none of the children ever sensed it. Each was treated as a full Son, Daughter, Brother, or Sister by everyone, including Gwyn, who also had his family at Min-Yr-Afon.

Childhood Memories and Mischief

The countryside around Min-Yr-Afon, with its rolling hills, dense woodlands, and meandering streams, was a natural playground for Gwyn and his cousins. Their days were filled with the kind of adventures that only a rural childhood can provide, each new day bringing with it endless possibilities for exploration and mischief. Gwyn, along with Glyn, Vincent, and Keith, formed an inseparable band of explorers, each adventure fostering a bond that would last a lifetime.

Gwyn's early escapades were often led by Vincent

and Keith, the more mischievous of the cousins. They would orchestrate grand plans, from building elaborate dens in the woods to orchestrating mock battles with sticks for swords and shields made from old barrel lids. Gwyn, with his inherent curiosity and a sense of responsibility toward his younger cousins, followed along enthusiastically, taking on a more protective role and ensuring their safety while they learned the unwritten rules of boyhood camaraderie and adventure.

Autumn in Pembrokeshire brought with it the apple harvest, a time of buzzy activity and community spirit. Gwyn and his cousins took great delight in helping with the harvest, although their assistance was often punctuated by apple-throwing skirmishes and the covert snatching of the juiciest fruits. Aunt Martha, aware of their antics, would feign sternness but often let out a chuckle at their apple-stained faces and sheepish grins.

Winter snow transformed the landscape into a wonderland of opportunity for the boys. They spent hours building snowmen, engaging in spirited snowball fights, and sledging down the village's steepest hills. Gwyn, with his quiet imagination, would sometimes wander off to make intricate snow sculptures, a testament to his creative spirit and attention to detail.

Spring and summer were marked by outdoor expeditions. The boys would go on long walks through the countryside, sometimes venturing as far as the neighbouring villages.

These journeys were not just for play; they were a rite of passage, teaching them about the land, its history, and the interconnectedness of the village communities. Gwyn, with his thoughtful nature, often found himself pondering the stories and legends of each place they visited.

Gwyn's childhood was not just about play; it was a time of learning and growth. Martha and Lewis, while providing a loving and stable home, encouraged the boys to learn practical skills. Gwyn learned to tend the garden, care for the small family livestock, and assist with minor repairs around the house. These tasks, though sometimes seen as chores, taught him responsibility and the satisfaction of contributing to the family's well-being.

As Gwyn grew older, the escapades of childhood gradually gave way to the responsibilities of adolescence. Yet, the memories of these carefree days remained etched in his mind, a reminder of the joys of youth and the unbreakable bonds formed with his cousins. These experiences, filled with laughter, adventure, and occasional mischief, laid the foundation for the resilient and adaptable young man Gwyn would become.

Shadows of War

As the 1920s progressed, the world outside the peaceful confines of Letterston and Min-Yr-Afon began to change in ways that the young Gwyn Morgan could scarcely understand. The aftermath of World War I had left deep scars across Europe, and the rumblings of political and social unrest were gradually building into what would become a prelude to another great conflict. These distant events, while seemingly remote, began to cast their shadows over the village, subtly shifting the conversations among adults and the stories shared at the local pub.

Gwyn, growing into a perceptive and thoughtful boy, could sense the change in the air. He overheard hushed conversations about political tensions in far-off lands, discussions of economic hardships, and whispers of rising leaders with unsettling ideologies. These snippets of adult talk, though cryptic to his young mind, instilled in him an awareness that the world was much larger and more complex than the boundaries of his village and the fields of Min-Yr-Afon.

The village itself, while still retaining much of its timeless charm, was not immune to the changes sweeping the globe. The local newspaper, once filled with stories of community events and local happenings, began to feature articles about national politics and international affairs. Uncle Lewis, who had served in the Great War, occasionally shared his thoughts on these developments, his tone reflecting a mix of concern and hope that the world would not tumble back into the chaos of conflict.

In the schoolhouse, Gwyn's lessons began to include more about the history and current events. His teacher, Mr. Davies, a veteran himself, often emphasized the importance of understanding history to avoid repeating its mistakes. These lessons left a profound impression on Gwyn, fostering in him a budding interest in world affairs and a deeper understanding of the sacrifices made during the war.

Despite these undercurrents of change, life in Letterston continued with its daily rhythms. The seasons came and went, the harvests were gathered, and community events were celebrated with the same enthusiasm as always. Yet, there was a growing sense that the world was inching towards something unknown and ominous. The adults, including Aunt Martha and Uncle Lewis, made efforts to shield the children from these concerns, but their efforts could not entirely mask the sense of apprehension that was slowly seeping into the community.

As the decade drew to a close, the impact of these global events began to be felt more tangibly in Letterston. Some families received news of relatives affected by the economic downturns or political upheavals in other parts of the country. Discussions about national defence and military service, once abstract concepts to Gwyn, became more frequent and carried a new weight and urgency.

Gwyn's understanding of these issues grew as he approached his teenage years. The playful innocence of his childhood was gradually being replaced by a more sombre awareness of the world's complexities. He began to ask more questions, seeking to understand the nature of the unrest and the reasons behind the looming threats.

His conversations with Uncle Lewis, once filled with tales of folklore and adventure, took on a more serious tone, as Gwyn sought to grasp the realities of war and its impact on people and nations.

As Chapter 1 closes, Gwyn stands on the threshold of adolescence, his childhood marked by love, loss, adventure, and the dawning realization of a world far larger and more complicated than he had ever imagined. The shadows of war, though still distant, were lengthening, hinting at the profound changes that were to come. In the safety of Min-Yr-Afon, surrounded by the love of his aunt, uncle, and cousins, Gwyn prepares to step into a future where the lessons of his past and the realities of a turbulent world would converge.

CHAPTER TWO

The Looming Threat

In the late 1930s, the dark clouds of war cast their ominous shadows over Europe. The idea of conflict haunted the collective consciousness, and the people of Letterston, like millions of others, couldn't escape the impending storm. The quaint village, nestled in the serene landscapes of Wales, had long enjoyed a tranquil existence, seemingly untouched by the political turmoil brewing beyond its borders. Yet, even in this remote corner of the world, the rumblings of impending catastrophe could not be ignored.

The world had learned painful lessons from the Great War, and the growing tension in Europe served as a grim reminder that peace was fragile. The headlines in the local newspaper, once filled with stories of community events and jovial gatherings, were now dominated by ominous news from abroad. Gwyn, now a teenager, found himself captivated by these reports, unable to avert his gaze from the headlines that screamed of international crises and political brinkmanship.

As the villagers congregated in the warm embrace of the village pub, conversations grew increasingly sombre. The regulars, many of them veterans who had survived the horrors of the trenches during World War I, now spoke of the looming threat with a mixture of gravity and solemnity. Their eyes, etched with the scars of past conflicts, conveyed the weight of their experiences as they shared their stories with the younger generation.

Gwyn, ever the attentive listener, absorbed their tales of bravery and sacrifice. He found himself hanging on to every word, the images of war painted by these veterans etching themselves into his young mind. Their stories weren't mere anecdotes; they were cautionary tales of the consequences of inaction and indifference.

In the evenings, as the sun dipped below the horizon, Gwyn often found himself gazing at the fading light and contemplating the uncertain future that lay ahead. The idyllic countryside, once a haven of peace, now seemed to hide the secrets of impending turmoil. The innocence of his childhood was gradually giving way to the harsh realities of a world on the brink of chaos.

The village of Letterston, with its cobblestone streets and thatched cottages, remained a picture of timeless beauty. But beneath its picturesque façade, a growing sense of apprehension took root. Gwyn, with his keen sense of observation and a thirst for knowledge, was increasingly drawn into the whirlwind of history. The looming threat, though still distant, was becoming an undeniable presence in the lives of the villagers, including Gwyn's, as they stood on the precipice of a new era filled with uncertainty and upheaval.

Enlistment and Early Training

In July 1939, as war clouds gathered, Gwyn received a letter that would change the course of his life. The call to service had come, and he was to report for a medical examination in Llanelli. The prospect of leaving his beloved village and family filled him with a mix of excitement and trepidation.

The letter arrived one morning, delivered by the village postman, who had become a familiar figure in Letterston, known by name to nearly everyone. Gwyn, still in his work-worn clothes from helping Uncle Lewis in the fields, opened the envelope with trembling hands. His heart raced as he read the official summons, each word a stark reminder that the world beyond the village was in turmoil.

As he shared the news with Aunt Martha, her face registered a complex array of emotions. She had watched Gwyn grow from a small, motherless boy into a responsible young man, and now the call to military service had come. Her eyes reflected a mixture of pride, concern, and a mother's enduring love. She knew that Gwyn was embarking on a path fraught with uncertainty, and her maternal instincts tugged at her heartstrings.

The news also reached the ears of Uncle Lewis, who had served in the Great War. He understood the weight of the decision Gwyn was about to make and the challenges that lay ahead. Lewis had experienced the hardships of military life firsthand, and he knew that the road ahead would be arduous. Yet, he offered his support, imparting words of wisdom about resilience, camaraderie, and the importance of looking out for one's comrades.

In the days that followed, Gwyn's preparations for departure were a flurry of activity. He sorted through his modest belongings, packing essentials and cherished mementoes of home. The realization that he would soon leave the familiar surroundings of Letterston weighed heavily on his heart. The thought of parting from Aunt Martha, Uncle Lewis, and his cousins filled him with a profound sense of loss.

The day of his departure for Llanelli arrived with a mix of emotions. Gwyn wore his best suit, a gesture of respect for the occasion. The journey to the medical examination was a sombre one, with Aunt Martha and Uncle Lewis by his side. The countryside, which had once been a canvas of beauty and wonder, seemed different now, as if it too, was aware of the gravity of the moment.

Arriving at the examination centre, Gwyn was met with a sea of young faces, all embarking on their own journeys of duty and sacrifice. The atmosphere was charged with a sense of purpose and resolve. As he underwent the medical examination, he couldn't help but wonder about the fate that awaited him.

The examination was thorough. The doctor recorded every detail of Gwyn's body. His height was registered at 5-foot-4 inches, his weight at 129 lbs. and his expanded chest girth at 34 inches. His appearance was recorded as a 'Fresh' complexion, with blue eyes and brown hair. The doctor performing the examination also recorded a scar that ran up the inside of his right leg and across the front of his left. Despite this, his physical condition was recorded as 'Good' and was assigned to the medical category of 'A1'. The best possible conditions, reserved for frontline soldiers.

Gwyn's enlistment was a moment of personal significance, but it also represented a collective response to the gathering storm. The call to service had resonated across generations, from those who had lived through the horrors of World War I to the young men like Gwyn, who were now stepping forward to defend their homeland and uphold the values of freedom.

As Gwyn's journey to military service began, he carried with him the love and support of his family, the wisdom of Uncle Lewis, and the lessons of his childhood in Letterston. The road ahead was uncertain, but he faced it with determination, knowing that he was part of a generation that would be defined by its courage and sacrifice in the face of an uncertain future.

Basic Training at Park Hall

Gwyn's journey into the world of military service continued as he embarked on his initial training at the 210th AA training battery, stationed at Park Hall, Oswestry, Shropshire. This phase of his military education would be a transformative experience, testing his physical endurance and mental resilience while forging deep bonds with fellow trainees.

Park Hall was taken over by the army in 1915 and used as a training camp and military hospital throughout the First World War. It was handed back to the Oswestry corporation in the 1920s and was used as a well-known motorcycle racetrack until the army reactivated the camp in July 1939 as a Royal Artillery training camp and plotting office.

Upon his arrival at Park Hall, Gwyn was greeted by the sprawling training facility, where the echoes of commands and the clatter of boots filled the air. The barracks, austere and regimented, became his new home. He exchanged the familiar comforts of Min-Yr-Afon for the strict discipline of military life, a transition that both challenged and reshaped his identity.

The training regimen was unrelenting, designed to prepare Gwyn and his fellow trainees for the demands of wartime service. Mornings began with the blare of reveille, signalling the start of another gruelling day. Physical fitness drills, with their punishing routines of callisthenics and long marches, tested the limits of endurance. Gwyn's body, accustomed to the rhythms of farm work and outdoor exploration, now faced the rigours of military conditioning.

The training extended beyond physical fitness, encompassing gunnery instructions and the intricacies of anti-aircraft defence. Gwyn absorbed these lessons with the same diligence he had exhibited in his studies back in Letterston. The knowledge he gained was not only a matter of personal growth but a vital contribution to the collective defence of his homeland.

Amidst the challenges, Gwyn found camaraderie among his fellow trainees. Bonds formed in the crucible of shared hardship, as they faced physical exhaustion, harsh weather, and the unyielding demands of their instructors. Together, they became a band of brothers, relying on each other for support and encouragement.

Evenings in the barracks brought a respite from the day's intensity, as Gwyn and his comrades shared stories, dreams, and a shared determination to excel in their training. The friendships forged during these moments became an enduring source of strength and motivation.

As weeks turned into months, Gwyn's transformation was evident. His physique had become lean and resilient, his endurance unmatched, and his understanding of anti-aircraft defence comprehensive. He had not only adapted to military life but had embraced it with a sense of purpose.

Transfer to the 280th Battery

Gwyn's journey through the world of military service took another crucial turn on the 13th of November 1939, as he received orders for a transfer to the 280th battery of the 87th Anti-Aircraft (AA) regiment. This transition marked a significant step in his military career, bringing with it new responsibilities, advanced training, and a heightened sense of duty.

The transfer to the 280th battery saw Gwyn being ordered to relocate to the Royal Artillery Barracks at Hebburn-on-Tyne, where he would be stationed in South Shields, a place teeming with industrial activity and bustling with the preparation for potential conflict. The Tyneside area, a hub of vital industries and infrastructure, required vigilant protection against the looming threat of aerial attacks. Gwyn's role would be intricately linked to the defence of this critical region.

In his new assignment, Gwyn would undergo a more specialized and advanced training regimen. He would delve deeper into the intricacies of anti-aircraft artillery and hone his skills in precision targeting and rapid response. The threats of enemy bombers would be ever-present, and Gwyn's ability to react swiftly and effectively would be paramount to the safety of the area.

Gwyn's days would be filled with rigorous drills, gunnery practice, and simulations of enemy air raids. His instructors would demand perfection and push him to the limits of his capabilities. Every shot to be fired in training would be a testament to his commitment to protect his country and the industrious communities it housed.

The transition to the 280th battery also meant that Gwyn would now be part of a larger, more complex operation. Teamwork and coordination would become vital aspects of his role. He would forge new bonds with fellow soldiers, learning to trust and rely on each other in the high-pressure environment of anti-aircraft defence.

Nights spent on alert would bring their own challenges. The wailing sirens and the distant drone of enemy aircraft would serve as a constant reminder of the ever-present danger. Gwyn and his comrades would stand watch, ready to spring into action at a moment's notice.

Gwyn's transfer to the 280th battery would mark a pivotal moment in his military career. He would evolve from a trainee at Park Hall into a seasoned soldier with a specialized skill set. His responsibilities would be clear, to protect the vital industrial heartland of Tyneside and to stand vigilant against the looming threat of aerial attacks.

CHAPTER THREE

Anti-Aircraft Defence

Prior to the Second World War, Britain's Anti-Aircraft defence system was hugely underdeveloped. So, in 1925 as the political situation began to look less favourable in Europe, Britain began to slowly develop the defensive system. At the beginning of 1925, there were 2 Anti-Aircraft brigades with around 5000 men defending the Island from enemy attack. But by 1936, these numbers had increased significantly, and 2 AA divisions had formed with around 25,000 soldiers in each. By 1938 there were 5 divisions and they formed 1 AA Corps, and in 1939 there were 7, with the Corps now becoming a command in charge of over 175,000 troops.

These numbers seemed enormous compared to those of the First World War, but any comparison would be invalid with the technological advances in aviation. This was confirmed only 8 months after the AA command was formed, when the Germans bombed Rotterdam killing over 30,000 people in only 30 minutes. In contrast, the 8 months of the blitz saw the loss of around 40,000 civilians. When you compare these horrific numbers, it helps to validate the development of the British Anti-Aircraft Command and its importance.

Despite the increase in trained Anti-Aircraft Gunners, the production of new or renovated guns was slow. This made the fact that only a year later, a fully armed, trained, and capable artillery was prepared to meet the deadly Luftwaffe, even more impressive.

The Guns and Their Positions

There were three main types of Anti-Aircraft guns used by the British during the war, there was the 4.5-inch gun that hurled huge shells that weighed almost 25 kgs to a ceiling height of around 44,000 feet. The second and by far the most commonly used, was the 3.7-inch gun that fired 13kg shells to around 41,000 feet, but at a much faster speed. There was also a 3-inch gun that fired to around 25,000 feet and its main characteristics were a high firing rate. These light Anti-Aircraft guns were used during the First World War and had become largely outdated as the speed and power of the 3.7-inch guns were far more versatile.

The 3.7-inch gun was the more popular option due to its quick rate of fire matched with its devastating power. These were manufactured and supplied to the military in 2 different specifications. The first was the static gun, which was mounted onto a travelling platform with removable wheels so that the gun could be fixed to a solid base, usually concrete. Later in the war, it was found that these could be mounted on a temporary platform made from railway sleepers and would work adequately whilst making them easy and quick to redeploy.

The second was a mobile gun mounted on a travelling platform with four wheels and four levelling jacks, one at each corner. These jacks could lift the gun and wheels off the ground, keeping the platform level and stable, and could be ready for action in only 15 minutes.

Both variants could rotate 360 degrees on their mounting and provide elevation up to 80 degrees. Both would be pulled slowly behind a heavy-duty 4x4 truck, usually an AEC Matador that became known as an Artillery tractor. The Artillery tractor could reach a maximum of 25 mph whilst loaded with guns that weigh well over eight tonnes. They were also rail mountable, which would be utilised for longer journeys.

These guns would be manned by gunners that made up teams, or batteries. Each battery would be made up of between 100-200 men or women and up to eight guns, usually of the same type to simplify the stores of ammunition and equipment. The battery would usually be divided into two separate teams of four guns each and placed in locations a mile or so apart with a centrally placed HQ. This made it more difficult for the enemy aircraft to avoid them due to their well-distributed range and reduced the risk of an air strike wiping out an entire battery in one attack.

The selection of a gun site was critical for its successful deployment. For the mobile gun in the field, reconnaissance units would scout ahead to find a site suitable to house these colossal weapons. The site must have no obstructions higher than 10 degrees and it must be defendable from the ground, so, machine gun posts in particular, must be possible. A site must also have good exit routes as they may be ordered to move at a second's notice. The administrative conveniences must also be considered, as access to water, electricity and telephone services was important.

Once the site has been selected, the reconnaissance unit would send for another unit, usually a pioneer or logistical unit, to move ahead of the battery and utilise any structure nearby to provide sufficient infrastructure for the incoming gunners. They would need some form of shed or hut to be used as a cookhouse, a semi-permanent structure, possibly a marquee, to be used as a battery office, and some tents or huts for eating and sleeping. Once these have been established, the guns and men could be brought forward to their makeshift home.

Once the men arrived, they would unpack their supplies, stores, ammunition, and guns, they would settle into their new sleeping quarters and take in a meal of some description. By the time they would wake in the morning to their miniature village, their reconnaissance unit would be reporting back, in an extraordinarily short amount of time, providing information about local amenities and conveniences that the men may be able to utilise during their downtime.

Over time, the structures are made more permanent and living conditions more comfortable. An office would be created for the communication and plotting office, sometimes in a stone structure sunk below the surface. Guns would be laid out evenly around the outskirts of the area with the command post at the center. The command post is the integral heartbeat of any gun site. Within it would be the predictor, the spotters, and the height finders. It would also be the home of the GPO (Gun position officer) who is responsible for the area.

The Life of a Gunner

Arriving at a gun site was a huge undertaking for the gunners. Their priority would be to create a flat site for their gun, and once that has been achieved, the gun is erected and levelled. The gunners would then get to work digging a pit around the gun with several recesses. Walls would slowly be built up around the pit with sandbags that would then be camouflaged with turf. These recesses would be used mainly for ammunition stores, but 1 is reserved as a shelter for the long nights that the battery is on alert and unable to leave their guns but are not needed at their positions. Here, the men would spend the cold nights dozing with one ear listening carefully for the alarm to sound.

Once these recesses had been dug, the task of storing their ammunition required a great amount of care. They were stored in long metal boxes, stacked in a methodical way that air could circulate around them. They would be separated by strips of timber that would prevent the boxes from ever touching. It was also the responsibility of the gunners to examine each box of ammunition every day to ensure it remained free of rust and condensation.

When an aircraft was detected, it would be the job of the plotter to identify the plane. If it is identified as a friendly aircraft, it would be noted in their logs, but if it is identified as hostile, the alarms would be raised. They would fix their sights on the aircraft and the GPO would read the height and bearing that would be displayed on the base of the telescope and call it out. This information would be fed to the gunners that were rushing to their stations. Continued updates would be called from the command post along with the predictor's estimate for the location that the gunners should aim. All of this would play out in the blink of an eye with no room for error.

The job of an Anti-Aircraft gunner was possibly one of the most underappreciated tasks of the war. An example of this was during a raid over the Widnes area in 1941, a lone AA battery scored a hit on an Heinkell which winged it and caused it to lose speed and altitude. An RAF fighter that was in the area picked up on the wounded aircraft and finished it off. The enemy crash-landed into a small playing field on the outskirts of town and burst into flames. The pilot perished in the inferno, but the 3 other crew members escaped the flames only to be captured. In this scenario, as with hundreds of others, the RAF fighter was credited with the success. Though this is a perfect example of the British defence working in unison, the task of those on the ground is sometimes overlooked. The stark truth is that fighter command would not have been as successful without the modest work of AA command.

The difficulty of attempting to hit an aircraft is

another matter. A field gun, sat in a stationary position, shooting a stationary target, mathematically, could have only expected to hit its target once per 100 rounds. With the AA guns, the aircraft they can hear overhead would still be around 2 miles away. They would need to calculate its speed, height and course before firing at an area almost 2 miles ahead of them, so 4 miles ahead of the aircraft. The plane could be travelling up to 300mph and was more than capable of performing evasive manoeuvres. So, the chances of a direct hit were slim, though not impossible. That is why it would be unfair to judge these batteries on the number of aircraft they would bring down alone.

Although the Luftwaffe showed no respect for the early defence system, it slowly realised that the gunners were formidable, and word spread amongst its pilots of the fierce nature of the onslaughts they could expect. The task of bombing a specific target sounded easy enough, but with the flurry of AA shells, they would need to move about to disguise their route and evade the explosions, making it difficult to line up their bombing target. Only the finest German pilots would be able to hold their nerve and remain consistently on course at the critical moment that they released their bombs. The job of the AA gunners therefore was not only to bring planes down but to feed the uncertainty and fear that the faint-hearted pilots felt. The job of deterring the enemy was equally as significant as that of fighter command. Although the first two years of the war saw the Anti-Aircraft gunners bring down more than 600 planes over Britain, the true measure of success would be the number of aircraft they deterred from hitting their targets. Their primary aim was to keep the enemy at a high altitude and stop them from maintaining a consistent line towards their target.

The RAF fighter pilots also complimented the Anti-Aircraft gunners as their barrage towards the enemy would help the fighters spot an aircraft. The issue, in this case, would be the fact that the British spitfire, with its superior speed and agility, made it difficult for the gunners to time the halt of their assault on the target once the RAF fighter was in the area. There was a risk that the fast-moving spitfire could move into the direct line of fire that was fired ahead of where each aircraft was predicted to be.

The physical challenge of shooting down enemy aircraft was difficult enough, but the psychological task was equally tough. The gun locations would usually be in a secluded spot far from the comforts of home. They would be cramped in makeshift barracks, sometimes with no windows or source of heat. During the initial stages of the war, members of these batteries would admit that the job was easier when they were under relentless attack. During times when the risk of raids was low, they would fill their days with monotonous tasks that barely kept them warm. All the while, maintaining the appearance of readiness. They had to appear to be keen and enthusiastic despite the day-to-day repetitiveness. It could be a lonely, secluded existence for these men.

CHAPTER FOUR

The Northeast

Gwyn was transitioning seamlessly into his role in the 280th battery, but the air in South Shields was thick with anticipation. The threat of actual combat loomed ever closer, and as each day passed, the emotional and mental preparations of Gwyn and his comrades intensified.

The training had been rigorous, but now it was time for a different kind of readiness. Gwyn and his fellow soldiers were acutely aware that the skills they had honed were not just for drills and simulations. The distant rumblings of war on the continent reminded them that they stood on the precipice of a new and perilous reality.

In the evenings, as the sun dipped below the horizon, Gwyn and his comrades often gathered in the barracks to talk, smoke, and reflect. Their conversations revealed a range of emotions – fear, resolve, uncertainty, and even moments of dark humour. They shared stories of their families back home, spoke of the lives they had temporarily left behind, and whispered about the uncertain future that lay ahead.

For Gwyn, the anticipation was a complex mix of emotions. He felt a profound sense of duty and commitment to his country and the people who depended on his vigilance. At the same time, the thought of facing the relentless onslaught of enemy aircraft was undeniably daunting. The bond he had formed with his comrades became a source of strength, a reminder that they were in this together, facing the same fears and uncertainties.

The knowledge that they were the last line of defence for Tyneside weighed heavily on Gwyn and his fellow soldiers. They had trained relentlessly to be prepared, but the reality of war often defied preparation. The anticipation gnawed at them, leaving an unspoken tension in the air.

As the days turned into weeks, Gwyn's thoughts often drifted back to his family in Letterston. He wondered about their safety and well-being, knowing that the world he had left behind had also changed. These thoughts were especially poignant when his brother, Owen, was concerned as he was serving in the Merchant Navy. Sailing across the globe, avoiding the deadly German battleships and U-boats. Letters from home were a lifeline, offering glimpses of the familiar and a sense of connection to the world he had temporarily left behind.

In this atmosphere of anticipation, Gwyn's resilience was tested not just in physical training but also in mental fortitude. He learned to channel his emotions into a steely resolve, a determination to protect his homeland and the people he cared about. The bond he shared with his comrades grew stronger, forged in the crucible of shared uncertainty.

Arrival in South Shields

The journey to the northeast was a profound transition, a metaphorical bridge between the tranquil vistas of Letterston and the industrially charged atmosphere of his new post. As Gwyn stepped off the train, the air itself felt different—a symphony of mechanical hums and rhythmic clangs replacing the pastoral melodies of his Welsh village. The cobblestone streets of Letterston, where time seemed to move at a leisurely pace, gave way to expansive shipyards and towering cranes that dominated the Tyneside skyline. This was a landscape of strategic importance, where every clang and hum echoed the urgency of a nation on the brink of war.

South Shields, strategically positioned to safeguard the vital industrial heartland of Tyneside, pulsed with a sense of purpose that transcended the routines of training. The quaint village pub of Letterston now felt like a distant memory as Gwyn navigated the bustling streets. Here, the faces of the people bore not just the weight of daily life but also the gravity of impending responsibility. The air was thick with anticipation, a feeling that resonated with the stark realization that Gwyn had stepped onto the frontline of defence, where the looming threat was not a speculative shadow but a tangible, imminent reality.

The barracks of the 280th bty, standing in stoic solidarity, welcomed Gwyn into a new chapter of his military service. The starkness of military life found fresh expression in the regimented routines and disciplined order that characterized the region. Each step within its confines felt like a solemn progression from the idyllic Min-Yr-Afon to a place of sterner purpose. The camaraderie that had blossomed at Park Hall faced a new test amidst the industrial clamour of South Shields, where the bonds forged in training would evolve to face the heightened challenges of frontline duty.

The commanding officers, their leadership reflecting the gravity of the mission at hand, welcomed the fresh recruits with a blend of formality and shared purpose. Briefings were intense, with every word underscoring the significance of their role in protecting the industrial area from potential air raids. Gwyn, absorbing the weight of his newfound responsibilities, witnessed the seamless transition from the sheltered cocoon of training to the reality of active duty. As each day began with the sun rising above the industrial landscape, shrinking the long shadows that were cast over unfamiliar ground, Gwyn stood poised to embrace every day as a testament to his commitment to defend, and perhaps, to sacrifice.

Duties and Daily Life

Gwyn's daily life at the 280th bty unfolded with the precision of a well-oiled machine. The routines, meticulously designed for war, began with the blare of reveille, echoing through the barracks and rousing soldiers to a new day of duty. Mornings were a flurry of activity, with the clatter of boots on the parade ground, the crisp salute of soldiers, and the distant echoes of commands cutting through the dawn air. Physical fitness drills, a relentless cascade of callisthenics and endurance training, tested the mettle of every soldier, reaffirming their bodies as instruments of defence.

The heart of Gwyn's duties lay in the meticulous maintenance of anti-aircraft artillery, each piece a sentinel standing guard against the prospect of aerial threats. The intricate dance of loading, aiming, and firing became second nature to him, a fusion of skill and muscle memory honed through rigorous training. Gwyn, once a farm boy navigating the gentle undulations of Welsh fields, now manoeuvred the complex machinery of war with a precision that mirrored the discipline instilled by his superiors.

Beyond the mechanical symphony of artillery maintenance, Gwyn's days were punctuated by theoretical sessions, where the intricacies of anti-aircraft defence were dissected and absorbed. Map readings and simulations became his companions, offering a glimpse into the unpredictable dance of wartime strategies. Each lesson, delivered with military precision, was a thread weaving into the fabric of Gwyn's understanding of his role in safeguarding Tyneside.

Amidst the rigours of duty, there were moments of respite—brief interludes where soldiers could exchange stories, share laughter, and find solace in the friendship born out of shared challenges. Evenings in the barracks became a sanctuary, a space where the weight of responsibilities momentarily lifted, replaced by the bonds of brotherhood.

The evenings, however, did not bring an end to vigilance. Nights were marked by sentry duties, where Gwyn and his comrades stood watch, eyes scanning the darkened skies for any sign of impending danger. The wailing sirens, the distant hum of aircraft engines, and the occasional blackout drills served as stark reminders that their training was not merely a rehearsal but a preparation for a reality that could unfold at any moment.

The mess hall, where soldiers gathered for sustenance, became another arena for the forging of bonds. Meals were not just a nutritional necessity but a communal affair, a time when soldiers shared not only food but also the burdens and triumphs of their duties. The clatter of cutlery against plates echoed the unspoken solidarity that bound these men together, each bite a testament to their shared commitment.

In this regimented existence, Gwyn found purpose. The daily grind, marked by routines that oscillated between physical exertion and intellectual engagement, moulded him into a guardian of the northeast. The relentless preparation, the forging of bonds, and the constant vigilance became threads woven into the tapestry of his life—a life defined by duty and an unwavering commitment to the defence of his country.

The Bonds of Brotherhood

In the crucible of military life at the 280th bty, Gwyn discovered a profound connection with his fellow soldiers that transcended the boundaries of comradeship. The barracks, once sterile and unfamiliar, transformed into a haven where the bonds of brotherhood were forged amidst the shared challenges and anticipation of the looming war.

Their camaraderie wasn't just a product of circumstance; it was a survival strategy, a source of strength in the face of an uncertain future. Gwyn found himself surrounded by men from diverse backgrounds, each carrying a unique story, yet all bound by the common purpose of defending Tyneside. In the shared mess hall conversations, he learned about their families, hometowns, dreams, and the variety of reasons that led them to wear the uniform. Laughter was an important part of this world. At a time when the air was filled with suspense and tension, there was always a strong need for the welcoming sound of fun. Jokes, both verbal and practical, were an everyday occurrence in their downtime, and part of the mental pause from their struggles.

The rigours of training and the constant awareness of their responsibilities created a unique camaraderie—one born out of mutual reliance and shared adversity. The physical and mental challenges they faced together forged bonds that went beyond the superficialities of everyday interactions. In each other, they found allies who understood the weight of duty and the sacrifices demanded by wartime service.

The bonds extended beyond the confines of duty. When one soldier faced a personal challenge, the collective strength of the brotherhood rallied to support him. The notion of "leave no man behind" was more than a motto; it was a creed that permeated their actions, reinforcing the idea that their survival and success were interdependent.

As the months passed, the initial camaraderie evolved into a brotherhood marked by an unspoken understanding. They had become more than a unit; they were a family, a collective force ready to face the challenges of war as one. Gwyn, once a lone farm boy from Letterston, now stood shoulder to shoulder with comrades turned brothers, united in their commitment to protect Tyneside —a brotherhood forged in the crucible of duty, shared sacrifice, and an unbreakable bond of trust.

First Encounter with the Enemy

The long-awaited moment finally arrived, ushering in a palpable shift in the atmosphere of South Shields. The tranquillity of routine shattered, replaced by the looming spectre of war materializing in the form of Gwyn's inaugural encounter with the enemy. The air itself seemed to crackle with tension, an electric charge of anticipation coursing through the barracks and permeating the night.

As intelligence reports hinted at a potential

enemy presence in the vicinity, the routine drills and simulated exercises that once felt like distant rehearsals now acquired a heightened significance. The reality of facing an actual threat transformed the meticulously trained responses into a reflexive dance of preparation, sending ripples of both apprehension and determination through the entire unit.

On that fateful January night, the world outside the barracks was draped in an eerie stillness, punctuated only by the distant hum of the Tyne River and the occasional rustle of leaves. Gwyn assumed his position as a sentinel, his gaze scanning the horizon for any signs of movement. The darkness seemed to cloak the impending danger, heightening the senses of every soldier on watch. The metallic scent of the sea hung in the air, and the distant city lights shimmered like distant stars, casting an otherworldly glow over the landscape.

Then, a crackling voice broke the silence, the radio relaying urgent information about unidentified aircraft approaching the Tyneside. The barracks erupted into controlled chaos as soldiers moved with swift precision to their positions, their training transforming the chaos into a choreographed display of readiness. Gwyn felt a surge of adrenaline as he secured his helmet, his hands moving with practised efficiency over the anti-aircraft equipment.

The night sky transformed into a theatre of uncertainty, punctuated by the shrill wail of air raid sirens. Gwyn's heart pounded in his chest as he trained his gaze on the heavens, searching for the ominous silhouettes of enemy aircraft. The collective breath of the unit seemed to pause, suspended in a moment pregnant with the gravity of impending conflict.

Then, the moment arrived. A distant rumble reverberated through the air, and shadowy figures emerged on the horizon. The tension peaked as the first salvo of enemy aircraft approached. The deafening roar of anti-aircraft fire erupted, a symphony of defiance against the encroaching threat. Tracer rounds streaked across the sky, painting ephemeral trails of light that danced in a deadly ballet.

As the first enemy planes came into view, Gwyn experienced a surreal mix of fear and determination. The training that once felt like a distant memory now manifested in a cacophony of orders, shouts, and the rhythmic thud of anti-aircraft guns. The night became a tempest of sound and fury, and Gwyn, along with his comrades, unleashed a storm of defensive fire against the intruders.

In that chaotic ballet of war, Gwyn's world narrowed to the sights and sounds of combat. The acrid smell of gunpowder mingled with the salt-laden breeze, and the night echoed with the percussive symphony of explosions. As the enemy planes retreated into the darkness, Gwyn stood amidst the aftermath, his body trembling with a potent cocktail of exhilaration and exhaustion. Though the enemy was deterred from trespassing over British airspace, the adrenaline that rushed through the men in the heat of the moment left them with the buzz of war and a practical understanding of the challenge of firing at a hostile aircraft. The plane, probably only on a reconnaissance task, hadn't fired a shot nor dropped a bomb, but the encounter had given the unit a taste of battle.

The first encounter with the enemy left an indelible mark on Gwyn and his comrades. The distant threat had become tangible, and the abstract notions of war transformed into a visceral reality. In the aftermath, as the echoes of conflict faded, Gwyn and his fellow soldiers found solace in the unspoken understanding that they had faced the enemy and emerged as a united force—a brotherhood tested and proven in the crucible of battle, forging bonds that transcended the mere camaraderie of soldiers.

Reflections and Resolutions

In the quiet aftermath of the first skirmish, Gwyn found himself contemplating the weight of his role in the defence of Tyneside. The barracks, once alive with the urgent energy of combat, now settled into a subdued stillness. The scent of gunpowder lingered, a tangible reminder of the recent clash against the unseen adversary. Gwyn's mind, however, was far from still; it churned with reflections on the journey from Letterston to the front lines of war.

As he stared out of the barracks window, the moon casting a silvery glow on the landscape, Gwyn couldn't escape the gravity of the responsibility that now rested squarely on his shoulders. The quaint village of Letterston seemed like a distant memory, a world untouched by the harsh realities of conflict. The bond with his family, the cobblestone streets, and the warmth of Aunt Martha's hearth—all felt like fragments of a bygone era. Yet, in this introspective moment, Gwyn recognized that these memories were the very foundation that fueled his resolve to protect.

Letters from home, the lifeline that connected him to the familiar, took on a newfound significance. Each word penned by Aunt Martha and the occasional drawings from his younger cousins became a source of comfort in the tumultuous sea of war. Gwyn clung to these missives, finding solace in the shared laughter and the descriptions of daily life in Letterston—a stark contrast to the harsh realities of the military landscape.

The camaraderie forged in the crucible of conflict became a pillar of support for Gwyn. The faces of his fellow soldiers, illuminated by the dull glow of barracks lanterns, held the shared experiences of the first encounter. The unspoken understanding among them transcended mere friendship, evolving into a brotherhood bound by a common purpose. The weight of duty was not a burden borne in isolation; it was a collective responsibility shared with those who stood shoulder to shoulder in the defence of their homeland.

As dawn painted the sky in hues of pink and gold, Gwyn's thoughts turned to the future. The war-torn landscape of Tyneside seemed to stretch endlessly, a canvas upon which the narrative of their collective resilience was still being written. The anticipation that once gripped him had evolved into a steely resolve. The first encounter had stripped away the veneer of romanticized notions about war, leaving behind a pragmatic understanding of its grim realities. Yet, within that understanding, Gwyn discovered a profound sense of purpose—to protect, to defend, and to ensure that the cobblestone streets of villages like Letterston remained untouched by the ravages of conflict.

In the barracks, where the air still hummed with the echoes of battle, Gwyn and his comrades affirmed their commitment. Their reflections weren't just personal; they were a mosaic of shared aspirations and collective determination. The war was not an abstract concept—it was the very air they breathed, the ground they defended, and the future they fought to secure. In the quiet resolve that bound them together, Gwyn found strength—a strength that transcended the individual and became a testament to the indomitable spirit of those who had been chosen as the guardians of the Tyneside.

CHAPTER FIVE

The Move to Middlesbrough

As Gwyn received orders for his transfer to Middlesbrough on the 22nd of January 1940, soon after his first taste of the enemy, the weight of strategic importance hung in the air. The bustling industrial hub, teeming with resources vital to the war effort, made Middlesbrough the first major town in Britain bombed by the Luftwaffe.

The urgency was palpable, the atmosphere charged with the awareness that this move placed him at the forefront of the conflict.

Middlesbrough, with its steelworks and shipyards, was not just a location but a linchpin in the defence against the Luftwaffe. Gwyn's posting in South Shields placed him on the last line of defence for the region, but Middlesbrough was the main target. Here, there would be no innocent reconnaissance flights. Here, the Luftwaffe came to kill.

Arriving in Middlesbrough, Gwyn couldn't escape the visible signs of war preparation. The town, once marked by the rhythm of industrial life, now bore the scars of anticipation. The steel behemoths stood as silent sentinels, and the air hummed with a different kind of energy. Gwyn's initial reactions were a mix of awe and trepidation. The gravity of his new role settled on his shoulders as he beheld the vastness of the industrial complex that was now under his watchful gaze. His time in the 280/87th AA was brief, as reorganisation meant a rapid transfer to the 175/85th AA only one day after arriving in Middlesbrough. However his position did not change, and he remained stationed at the same barracks.

His responsibilities in Middlesbrough required a swift adaptation to the heightened stakes of defending such a critical location. The training and drills became more intense, reflecting the urgency of the situation. Gwyn and his unit underwent a rigorous routine, each day preparing for the imminent threat of Luftwaffe attacks. The air crackled with tension, mirroring the anticipation that permeated every corner of the city. Gwyn's transformation into a guardian of Middlesbrough was underway, and the weight of the responsibility sat heavily on his shoulders.

Though South Shields introduced Gwyn to the reality of enemy contact, it was Middlesbrough that opened his eyes to the horror of enemy bombardment. This first major air raid marked a defining moment in Gwyn's experience in Middlesbrough. The wail of sirens and the distant drone of enemy aircraft painted an ominous picture. The city, once a beacon of industrial might, now became a target. The chaos and fear that unfolded during the raid tested Gwyn's training and resolve. As the Luftwaffe struck, the night sky turned into a canvas of destruction, and Gwyn found himself in the crucible of combat. The experience was a baptism by fire, forging his mettle in the heat of battle.

As the dust settled and the echoes of the raids faded, the men of the 175th bty leaned on each other for support. The relationships among the soldiers became a source of strength, a testament to the resilience of the human spirit in the face of adversity.

Amidst the ruins left by the Luftwaffe's onslaught, Gwyn stood as a witness to the devastation. The once-thriving city now bore the scars of war, and the emotional toll weighed heavily on his shoulders. The reflection amidst the ruins was not just physical but a deep introspection into the cost of war. Gwyn grappled with the harsh realities, questioning the price paid by both soldiers and civilians in the name of freedom and defence.

The move to Middlesbrough had transformed Gwyn's role from a guardian of the industrial heartland to a frontline defender against enemy attacks. The strategic importance of the location heightened the stakes, and as he settled into his new responsibilities, he faced the visceral realities of war with a determination to protect and preserve amidst the chaos.

Adapting to a New Role

As Gwyn settled into his new role in Middlesbrough, the weight of responsibility bore down on him. The transition demanded not only a physical relocation but also a mental adaptation to the heightened stakes of defending such a critical industrial hub. The routines and drills that unfolded in the wake of his arrival were emblematic of the urgency of the situation. Each day brought forth new challenges, and Gwyn found himself immersed in a relentless cycle of preparation for the inevitable Luftwaffe attacks that lay in the near future.

The industrial landscape of Middlesbrough became the backdrop to Gwyn's transformation into a guardian of the city. The once-familiar rhythms of farm life in Letterston were replaced by the relentless pulse of war preparation. The towering steelworks and bustling shipyards were not just symbols of industrial might but also potential targets in the escalating conflict. Gwyn's role required a deepened understanding of the intricacies of anti-aircraft defence, precision targeting, and rapid response—skills that were now honed to a razor's edge.

His unit underwent specialized training, drilling down into the nuances of defending against air raids. The urgency of their mission was reinforced by the constant awareness that the Luftwaffe could strike at any moment. Gwyn's adaptation to this new role wasn't just a matter of mastering technical skills; it was a psychological adjustment to the ever-present threat that loomed overhead. The training became more than routine; it was a lifeline, a means of survival in the face of an unpredictable enemy.

The heightened stakes demanded a level of camaraderie and cohesion among Gwyn and his comrades that surpassed anything experienced before. The bonds forged in the crucible of shared hardship deepened, as they relied on each other for support and encouragement. The shared sense of purpose became a unifying force, transcending individual differences and backgrounds. As they adapted to their new roles, the importance of teamwork and trust became evident in every drill and exercise.

The city's heartbeat echoed with the constant

drills and preparations. The urgency of defending Middlesbrough against potential Luftwaffe attacks permeated every aspect of Gwyn's daily life. The barracks, once a place of respite, now buzzed with a different energy— an energy fueled by the collective determination to protect their home. Gwyn's adaptation to this new role wasn't just about individual readiness; it was about fitting seamlessly into a well-oiled machine where each cog played a crucial part in the defence of the city.

The heightened sense of responsibility was not lost on Gwyn. As he adapted to his new role, he understood that the fate of Middlesbrough rested, in part, on his shoulders. The weight of this realization was both burdensome and motivating. It fueled his commitment to excellence, pushing him to go beyond the expected, to be not just a defender but a guardian of the city's future. The industrial might of Middlesbrough wasn't just a backdrop; it was the very essence of what they were defending.

The nights became a canvas for refining their skills and testing their readiness. The drills extended into the darkness, a stark reminder that the enemy could strike under the cover of night. Gwyn's adaptation to this new role wasn't confined to daylight hours; it was a 24/7 commitment to vigilance. As the air raid sirens wailed during their nocturnal exercises, Gwyn felt the gravity of his responsibilities acutely. The darkness became both an ally and a foe, concealing their movements while heightening the sense of vulnerability.

In adapting to his new role, Gwyn found a reservoir of strength within himself. The relentless training, the camaraderie, and the awareness of the city's dependence on their vigilance moulded him into a guardian of Middlesbrough. The adaptation wasn't just about surviving; it was about thriving in a role that demanded resilience, precision, and unwavering dedication. As he stood on the precipice of potential conflict, Gwyn's adaptation became a testament to the indomitable spirit of those who stood ready to defend against the encroaching shadows of war.

The Luftwaffe Strikes

GWYN – THE LIFE OF AN UNSUNG SOLDIER

The day Middlesbrough faced the wrath of the Luftwaffe was etched into Gwyn's memory with indelible ink. The air hung heavy with tension as the city braced for the impending storm. The distant hum of aircraft engines gradually grew louder, signalling the approach of an enemy force determined to rain destruction upon their industrial stronghold. Gwyn and his comrades, stationed in anticipation, felt a surge of adrenaline as the first ominous shadows of enemy planes darkened the skies.

The barrage began with an ear-splitting symphony of explosions, shattering the relative calm that had prevailed until then. The air raid sirens wailed in mournful harmony, a haunting melody that underscored the severity of the threat. Gwyn, amidst the chaos, felt the weight of his training pressing upon him—the drills, the simulations—all converging into this moment of truth. The city, once bustling with life, now cowered under the relentless assault from above.

The night illuminated with the hellish glow of anti-aircraft fire as Gwyn's unit sprang into action. The sky became a battleground, streaked with tracer rounds and punctuated by the distant roar of falling bombs. The cacophony of war drowned out all other sounds, and Gwyn's senses heightened as he focused on his role in this deadly dance. The Luftwaffe, realizing they faced formidable resistance, intensified their attack, unleashing a relentless torrent of bombs upon Middlesbrough.

In the heart of the storm, Gwyn felt a strange blend of fear and determination. The adrenaline coursing through his veins wasn't just a response to danger; it was a surge of purpose, a commitment to defend against the onslaught. Amidst the chaos, he glimpsed the faces of his comrades, each one a beacon of shared resolve amidst the turmoil. The bonds forged in training now held strong against the relentless tide of enemy fire.

The devastation unfolded with ruthless efficiency. Factories and homes crumbled under the impact of bombs, and the once vibrant cityscape transformed into a surreal landscape of destruction. Gwyn, though prepared for the brutal reality of war, couldn't suppress the shock of witnessing the city he had vowed to protect, succumb to the merciless assault. The Luftwaffe's strikes left scars on both the physical and emotional terrain of Middlesbrough.

As the air raid subsided, a heavy silence settled over the city. The acrid scent of smoke and burning debris hung in the air, a grim reminder of the cost of war. Gwyn surveyed the aftermath, grappling with a mixture of grief and resilience. The Luftwaffe had struck, but Middlesbrough had not crumbled. The indomitable spirit of the defenders, though tested, endured. In the eerie calm that followed the storm, Gwyn and his comrades regrouped, their bonds strengthened by the shared experience of facing the enemy head-on.

The aftermath of the air raid brought into sharp relief the toll of war on both infrastructure and human lives. Gwyn, as a guardian of Middlesbrough, faced the stark reality that protecting the city meant confronting the harsh consequences of conflict. The once-bustling streets were now laden with rubble and debris, and the survivors emerged from shelters with haunted expressions. In the ruins, Gwyn found a renewed resolve—the Luftwaffe's strikes had not broken their spirit but had ignited an unyielding determination to rebuild and resist.

As the sun rose over the battered city, Gwyn and his comrades stood amidst the wreckage, their faces etched with a mix of exhaustion and defiance. The Luftwaffe had struck, but Middlesbrough endured. The scars of that night would forever mark Gwyn's journey, a testament to the sacrifices made in the crucible of war. The Luftwaffe's strikes, though devastating, had only strengthened the resolve of those who stood as guardians of Middlesbrough.

Comradeship in Crisis

In the aftermath of the Luftwaffe's relentless assault on Middlesbrough, Gwyn and his comrades found themselves bonded not only by the shared experience of facing the enemy but also by the crucible of crisis. The air raid had tested their mettle, and in its aftermath, a unique camaraderie emerged among the soldiers who had stood shoulder to shoulder in defence of their city.

As the echoes of explosions faded, Gwyn and his comrades surveyed the cityscape now scarred by the ravages of war. The once-thriving neighbourhoods lay in ruins, and the survivors, emerging from shelters with a mix of relief and grief, bore witness to the toll of the Luftwaffe's strikes. In this desolate landscape, the bonds among the soldiers deepened. Each shared glance, every word exchanged, became a silent acknowledgement of the collective sacrifice made in the crucible of crisis.

The camaraderie wasn't confined to the battlefield alone; it extended into the mundane routines of daily life amidst the rubble. Gwyn and his comrades, now tasked with the dual responsibilities of defending and rebuilding, found solace in the shared burdens and responsibilities. Whether clearing debris, aiding survivors or standing watch for potential follow-up attacks, they forged a brotherhood in the crucible of crisis.

The barracks, once a place of respite and camaraderie, took on a deeper significance in the wake of the air raid. Gwyn and his comrades gathered in the shadow of destruction, their conversations reflecting both the gravity of the situation and a shared determination to persevere. The camaraderie that blossomed in the aftermath became a source of strength, a reminder that, even in the darkest times, they were not alone.

In the quiet moments between rebuilding efforts, Gwyn and his comrades shared stories of home, of families left behind, and of dreams for a future beyond the spectre of war. The human connection, amid the ruins, provided a glimmer of normality—a reminder that, despite the chaos, they were bound by something more profound than duty. This shared humanity became a beacon of hope, a resilient thread woven through the fabric of their camaraderie.

The trials they faced weren't solely physical; the emotional toll of witnessing the devastation weighed heavily on each soldier. Gwyn, in the company of his comrades, found a space to share these burdens. In the unspoken understanding that transcended words, they provided support and solace to one another, acknowledging the emotional wounds inflicted by the chaos of war.

As the city slowly rose from the ashes, so did the bonds among Gwyn and his fellow soldiers. The shared experience of crisis forged a unity that transcended the hierarchical structure of the military. Officers and enlisted men stood as equals, united by a common purpose—to protect, to rebuild, and to stand resilient in the face of adversity. The camaraderie born in crisis became a testament to the human spirit's capacity to endure, adapt, and find strength in unity.

The once-broken city of Middlesbrough became a canvas for collective resilience. Gwyn and his comrades, bound by the crucible of crisis, worked tirelessly to restore a semblance of normality to the lives shattered by war. Amidst the ruins, the bonds of brotherhood deepened, transforming a group of soldiers into a cohesive force driven not only by duty but by an unwavering commitment to one another.

In the face of ongoing challenges, Gwyn and his comrades drew strength from the camaraderie forged in crisis. The shared laughter amidst the debris, the silent nods of understanding, and the mutual reliance on one another became the pillars that supported their collective resilience. As Middlesbrough stood on the path to recovery, the soldiers, bound by the crucible of crisis, emerged not just as defenders of the city but as a tight-knit brotherhood whose bonds had been tested and proven unbreakable.

Reflections Amidst Ruins

In the sombre aftermath of the devastating Luftwaffe air raid on Middlesbrough, Gwyn found himself amidst the ruins of a city that had once thrived with life and industry. The landscape, now a chaotic tapestry of destruction, echoed with the haunting whispers of a war that had brought relentless havoc to the doorstep of the resilient community. Amidst the rubble and remnants of shattered buildings, Gwyn couldn't escape the visceral impact of the war—a war that had transformed not only the physical environment but also the collective psyche of those who called Middlesbrough home.

As the dust settled, revealing the harsh reality of the destruction, Gwyn stood amidst the ruins, contemplating the profound toll of conflict. The once-familiar streets, now unrecognizable, bore witness to the fragility of human achievement in the face of war's indiscriminate wrath. The skeletal remains of buildings reached desperately towards the sky, silent reminders of the lives disrupted, and dreams shattered.

The air was thick with the acrid scent of charred debris and the palpable weight of loss. Gwyn, along with his fellow soldiers, surveyed the desolation, grappling with a sense of helplessness in the face of such overwhelming destruction. The ruins stood as a testament to the destructive power of war, leaving an indelible mark on the landscape and the hearts of those who called Middlesbrough their home.

Amid the ruins, Gwyn's mind journeyed back to Letterston, the serene village that had once been his haven. He couldn't help but draw parallels between the innocence of his childhood and the harsh realities of war that now surrounded him. The war, once a distant threat, had carved its way into the very fabric of his existence, leaving an indelible mark on the landscape of his memories.

The remnants of daily life—crumbled storefronts, twisted lampposts, and fragments of personal belongings—whispered stories of ordinary people caught in the crossfire of global conflict. Gwyn couldn't escape the haunting realization that, behind each piece of debris, there was a narrative of resilience, survival, and, in some cases, tragic loss. The ruins bore witness to the human cost of war, forcing Gwyn to confront the profound impact of his role as a defender of the city.

Amidst the desolation, Gwyn sought solace in the camaraderie of his fellow soldiers. Their shared glances, laden with unspoken understanding, spoke volumes about the emotional toll they collectively bore. The ruins became a canvas for shared reflections, as soldiers grappled with the weight of responsibility, the cost of war, and the unyielding determination to rebuild amidst the destruction.

The stark contrast between the once-vibrant city and its current state heightened Gwyn's awareness of the impermanence of human achievements. The war, with its indiscriminate fury, had erased the familiar landmarks and replaced them with a landscape of brokenness. In the face of such devastation, Gwyn found himself questioning the very nature of the conflict and the toll it exacted not only on the physical world but on the souls of those who endured its trials.

Yet, amidst the ruins, Gwyn glimpsed signs of resilience and hope. The citizens of Middlesbrough, alongside the soldiers who stood as their guardians, began the arduous task of rebuilding. The ruins became a canvas for collective determination, a symbol of the unwavering spirit that refused to be extinguished. Gwyn, with a renewed sense of purpose, joined the efforts to reconstruct not just the physical structures but also the shattered dreams and aspirations that lay buried beneath the debris.

As the sun dipped below the horizon, casting a warm glow on the scarred cityscape, Gwyn couldn't help but feel a profound sense of responsibility. The ruins, though poignant in their portrayal of destruction, also carried the promise of renewal. The reflections amidst the ruins fueled Gwyn's commitment to safeguarding not just the physical safety of Middlesbrough but also the resilience of its spirit—a spirit that refused to be defined by the scars of war but instead found strength in the collective determination to rise again.

CHAPTER SIX

Call to Duty in the Continent

In the quiet confines of the barracks in the northeast, Gwyn received the orders that would alter the course of his wartime journey yet again. The call to duty in the Continent reverberated through the air, a summons that carried the weight of imminent peril. The urgency in the commanding officer's voice mirrored the gravity of the situation, signalling a pivotal moment in the unfolding drama of World War II.

Gwyn, now seasoned by his experiences in Tyneside & Teeside, felt a surge of mixed emotions.

The prospect of facing the enemy on the European mainland brought palpable tension to the air. The camaraderie among his fellow soldiers, forged in the crucible of training and anticipation, took on a new significance as they prepared for the unknown challenges that awaited them.

As he packed his kit, Gwyn couldn't shake the memories of the veterans in the Letterston pub, their tales of the Great War echoing in his mind. The call to duty stirred echoes of history, a reminder that the tranquil landscapes of Wales were intertwined with the broader tapestry of conflict. Gwyn, fuelled by a sense of duty and a determination to protect his homeland, prepared himself for the arduous journey that lay ahead.

The journey to the Continent began at Camberley in Surrey, where two specially commissioned military trains departed for Southampton at 1200 hrs. on the 4th of April 1940. The journey was a blend of anticipation and trepidation until finally embarking on the RMS Lady of Mann in Southampton at 1400 Hrs. along with 59 officers and 1226 other troops. Although now finally aboard the Lady of Mann, their journey still couldn't begin until they were collected by a convoy of four other ships at 0100 hrs. on the 5th of

April.

The crossing was smooth and uneventful as though the late spring weather was unaware of the hell that those aboard were about to face. They docked at Le Harve and were served breakfast on board before disembarking at 0830 hrs. As they stepped off the ship, rows of military trucks lined up along the quay waiting for the troops to board. Once packed into the back of one of these trucks, Gwyn began his journey to Boulleville where he would then be marched onwards to Lanquetot. Once there, he would be reunited with his precious AA gun, that had arrived the day before.

The landscape changed as they crossed borders and entered the theatre of war. The once serene countryside transformed into a theatre of strategic importance, where every hill and valley held the potential for skirmishes that would echo through history. Gwyn's senses heightened, attuned to the sounds of distant artillery and the hum of military vehicles that now surrounded him.

Arriving at the deployment site in Allery at 0800 hrs. on the 7th of April, Gwyn and his comrades were met with the stark reality of the frontlines. The bustling activity, the constant stream of orders, and the palpable tension in the air created a backdrop of controlled chaos. The call to duty was no longer an abstract concept; it was the very air they breathed, the pulse of an army gearing up for the impending clash.

Gwyn's initial impressions of the Continent were a mix of awe and foreboding. The historic landscapes, once celebrated for their cultural richness, now bore the scars of conflict. The weight of history pressed upon him as he walked on soil that would soon be contested in the theatre of war. The beauty of the landscape was overshadowed by the sense of impending battles, and Gwyn, a guardian of Tyneside & Teeside, was now a participant in a broader struggle for freedom.

The 175 bty's guns arrived by rail at the train station in nearby Arras, where Gwyn and his fellow AA gunners collected them, in the warm spring sunshine, en route to their gun position at Bullecourt. Whilst at Bullecourt, uncertainty as to what was to come in the Low Countries caused problems for the planning of the regiment. Discussions were had regarding a potential move to Norway, but a decision was made instead to order the 175th Bty to switch positions with the 16th AA Bty near Douai on the 7th of May.

During this spell near Douai, Gwyn experienced his first real success as an Anti-Aircraft gunner on the continent. At 0430 hrs. on the 10th of May, whilst manning his gun, a Luftwaffe raid was spotted on the horizon. As the low-flying enemy aircraft approached, Gwyn and his battery were fully submerged in the well-drilled dance of loading, aiming, and firing, when they landed a deadly hit on a Heinkell MKIII, bringing it crashing down. This was the first enemy aircraft brought down by the 1st Anti-Aircraft Brigade since the beginning of the war.

The Battlefront in Belgium

The highs of that early morning action suddenly turned into anxiety and trepidation at 0700 hrs. Gwyn enjoyed a brief respite in the barracks when news broke on the French wireless that Germany had invaded Belgium. Word around the barracks quickly spread as Belgium's neutrality had been broken, the BEF would now be permitted to enter the country, bringing them in direct contact with the German forces. As early as 0800 hrs. plans were being drawn up for the advance into Belgium. This became known as Plan D.

Their planned move into Belgium was scheduled

for 0700 hrs. on the 11th of May but was postponed by six hours due to the delay in reconnaissance. At 1400 hrs. they were finally given the green light to advance. They were led by J.R Stanton to their gun position near Stormbeek, north of Brussels and by 1200 hrs. on the 12th of May, they had arrived and were ready for action.

The transition from the quiet barracks of Tyneside & Teeside to the bustling battlefront in Belgium marked a stark shift in Gwyn's wartime narrative. As his boots touched the soil of this embattled European nation, the gravity of the situation became all-encompassing.

The strategic importance of Belgium was not lost on Gwyn. The quaint villages and historic towns now stood as strategic waypoints, each street and alley potentially holding the key to victory or defeat. The echoing footsteps of his fellow soldiers, the rumbling of military vehicles, and the distant thunder of artillery created a symphony of war that resonated through the Belgian countryside.

Gwyn's responsibilities on the battlefront demanded a heightened sense of vigilance. The enemy was not an abstract concept; it was a tangible force that lurked beyond the horizon. As he and his comrades took positions, the anticipation of the impending clash hung in the air like an unspoken truth.

The battlefront in Belgium was a canvas of uncertainty, and Gwyn, armed with the training and resilience instilled in him, was prepared to face the challenges head-on.

During the field battles that would consume Europe, Anti-Aircraft batteries like Gwyn's would be positioned at assembly points just behind the front line to provide aerial cover from the Luftwaffe, who would attempt to establish aerial superiority over the battle. Though out of range of enemy artillery, the fluidity of war, and the advance and withdrawal of the opposing sides would regularly bring close contact with the German ground forces.

The first face-to-face encounters with the enemy were a blend of chaos and clarity. The crackling of gunfire, the acrid scent of smoke, and the urgent shouts of commands painted a vivid picture of the battlefield. Gwyn's training kicked in, and amidst the turmoil, he navigated the challenges with a determination forged in the crucible of his military education. The Battlefront in Belgium was not just a physical battleground; it was a test of character and resilience. As Gwyn and his comrades fought on, the Belgian landscape bore witness to the ebb and flow of conflict. Villages changed hands, strategic positions shifted, and the very geography seemed to be reshaped by the tide of war. The Battlefront in Belgium was a dynamic theatre, and Gwyn, now a guardian of foreign soil, played his part in the intricate dance of warfare.

Nights on the battlefront brought a different kind of challenge. The darkness was punctuated by sporadic bursts of gunfire and the distant glow of explosions. Gwyn, like countless soldiers before him, found solace in the brief moments of respite. The camaraderie deepened as they shared stories in hushed tones, finding comfort during uncertainty. Gwyn's reflections amid the ruins of once-thriving towns revealed the toll of war on both the landscape and the human spirit. The juxtaposition of beauty and devastation painted a poignant picture, and as Gwyn gazed at the horizon, he knew that the battle was not just for land but for the ideals that defined their struggle.

The Withdrawal to Dunkirk

The intensity of the German onslaught began to overwhelm the Allied forces and strategic withdrawals were ordered. On the 17th of May at

1430 hrs. the 175th Bty were ordered to withdraw to Oudenaarde, around 50 miles west of Brussels. However, at 2230 hrs. the withdrawal routes became increasingly congested with refugees and the withdrawing frontline infantry. Due to this, the 175th bty were ordered to halt their own withdrawal to cover the infantry that passed through them from enemy aircraft. Seeing the battle-scarred faces of those ally soldiers that withdrew with horror etched in their eyes, only encouraged Gwyn and his fellow gunners to fight on with a desperation to protect them. The screaming sound of the dive bombers and the rhythmic drones of the machine guns became the soundtrack of the battle, and the horrors of dying women and children being desperately dragged from danger became the sights that Gwyn would remember.

They continued fighting heroically until 0100 hrs. on the 18th when the final infantry units had been withdrawn. Having completed their objective, they continued to Oudenaarde and arrived by 0830 hrs. Their time in Oudenaarde was brief as their delayed arrival meant plans for further withdrawal had already been drawn up, and by 1200 hrs. they were ordered to withdraw to Bellegem, just north of the French border near Lille.

On route to Bellegem, the convoy that Gwyn was a part of was violently attacked by low-flying Luftwaffe aircraft. The enemy aircraft sprung from the horizon without any warning and furiously machine-gunned the convoy. The sudden attack meant there was no chance of getting the AA guns operational, so whilst taking cover, they had nothing but rifle fire to deter the attack. Miraculously, the German attack was driven off without causing a single Allied casualty.

Having luckily escaped catastrophe, the 175th bty continued with their withdrawal and managed to arrive, unscathed, at Bellegem at 2230 hrs. When they arrived, billets (usually a private dwelling ordered to accept soldiers) had already been secured at a farm outside the town where the men slept in the barn, and the officers slept in the farmhouse. Gwyn took the opportunity to enjoy some well-earned rest in the relative safety of the barn, cushioned with plentiful amounts of straw to rest his exhausted body on. This was not only an opportunity for the troops to rest their battered bodies but also to take a psychological break from the emotional challenge of continuously being hunted by the enemy.

Following a much-needed night's rest, dawn broke

to the usual hum of military preparations until 0830 hrs. when plans were announced to recce an area for a new front line, where they hoped to regroup and halt the withdrawal. The unit was ordered to a crossroads between Wavrin and Lens, in the search for this stronghold on French soil. However, plans for this were quickly dismissed and orders were made for their continued withdrawal to Wavrin. The withdrawal orders continued as the 175th bty were ordered to Ploegsteert, northwest of Lille on the 21st, and then to Dunkirk on the 23rd.

The days leading up to the final withdrawal to Dunkirk were a whirlwind of orders and missions. Each hour was consumed by troublesome cries and situations that led to chaos. It was only when the panicked search for a footing on French soil was mentioned that Gwyn and his unit were made aware of their situation. They knew nothing of the encroaching German army that was rapidly encircling them. The congested roads and the brash orders of their commanding officers suggested there was an ominous cloud of doom encroaching, but the severity of the cloud had only just been realised.

As the echoes of battle reverberated through the Belgian and French landscape, the strategic imperative for a withdrawal to Dunkirk unfolded before Gwyn and his comrades. The decision to retreat was not a sign of defeat but a calculated move, a chess game played on the vast board of war. The once vibrant towns and villages, now scarred by conflict, witnessed the organised withdrawal of Allied forces, a symphony of strategic movements orchestrated in the face of adversity. Gwyn's role in the strategic withdrawal was defined by a sense of discipline. The order to retreat was met with a sombre acknowledgement of the challenges that lay ahead. The Battlefront in Belgium and France, once a theatre of confrontation, now transformed into a carefully choreographed withdrawal. The streets, once filled with the clamour of conflict, now echoed with the disciplined footsteps of retreating soldiers.

The journey to Dunkirk was fraught with challenges. The roads, marked by the scars of war, posed logistical hurdles that tested the mettle of Gwyn and his comrades. The strategic withdrawal was not a chaotic rout but a testament to the coordinated efforts of Allied forces. Gwyn's training, homed in the crucible of earlier battles, now played a pivotal role as they navigated the changing landscape and adapted to the fluidity of warfare.

Dunkirk, with its iconic beaches and the sprawling sea beyond, became the backdrop for one of the most remarkable events of World War II. The strategic withdrawal culminated in a desperate bid for evacuation, a race against time and the encroaching enemy forces. Gwyn and his comrades, now part of a vast assembly of soldiers, awaited their turn on the beaches, each minute laden with the uncertainty of survival.

CHAPTER SEVEN

Dunkirk Evacuation

The evacuation at Dunkirk unfolded as a colossal undertaking, a desperate bid to rescue hundreds of thousands of Allied soldiers stranded on the beaches of northern France. Gwyn, amidst the chaos and confusion, found himself thrust into the heart of this historic event. The vastness of the operation, encompassing naval vessels, civilian boats, and military ingenuity, spoke to the urgency of the situation and the perils that loomed over the stranded troops.

The beaches, once a symbol of military strategy,

now became a stage for the unfolding drama of survival. Gwyn and his comrades, battered by the relentless German advance, sought refuge along the coastline. The sprawling beaches, littered with abandoned equipment and the debris of war, bore witness to the magnitude of the evacuation. Against this backdrop, the evacuation efforts took shape, a testament to the determination to rescue as many men as possible from the clutches of the advancing enemy.

Gwyn and his battery proceeded to Dunkirk at 1015 hrs. on the 23rd of May, arriving at 2000 hrs. Once there, the 175th Bty HQ was established at Leffrinckoucke, just northeast of Dunkirk. Once established and the brigade had consolidated, it was realised that the entire brigade had only twenty-eight rounds of 3.7-inch AA ammunition remaining, which underlined the severity of the situation. From the time Gwyn arrived at Dunkirk, it was clear how heavily it had been, and still was being attacked. The beaches were bombed day and night by the Luftwaffe, engulfing the refinery and any tankers in the area. The constant rhythms of machine gun fire and the heart-stopping groan of the dive bombers allowed no respite.

On the 25th of May, Brigadier Bradwick took charge

of the defence surrounding the beaches and immediately drew up plans to hold off the Germans long enough to evacuate as many men from the French coast as possible. At 1300 hrs. Brigadier Bradwick designated specific gun positions for both 174th and 175th batteries, with Gwyn's 175th moving to Fort Mardyck. Brigadier Bradwick also informed the regiment of the serious position that the BEF had found themselves in and insisted that the Anti-Aircraft guns must remain in action at all costs, in order to protect the pocket of evacuation. To highlight the importance of this order, Bradwick arranged for delivery of 3.7-inch AA ammunition that arrived by 1430 hrs. that same day. It was delivered to Dunkirk by the SS Sandhill, who managed to unload the ammunition before being bombed and sunk by the Luftwaffe before being able to escape the chaos.

The fresh ammunition allowed Gwyn to continue his defence of Dunkirk with the fierce intensity that was needed. In a rare moment of joy, at 1430 hrs. on the 26th, the Luftwaffe resorted to propaganda, dropping thousands of leaflets. The comical leaflets displayed a map of Dunkirk highlighting the small Allied pocket that had been surrounded. Below the image of the map it read,

*"Look at this map: it gives your true situation!
Your troops are entirely surrounded – Stop fighting!
Put down your arms!"*

This caused much amusement amongst the men. After weeks of fighting toe to toe with such a relentless force, the thought of surrender courtesy of a simple flyer seemed amusing.

Final Retreat

By 2300 hrs. on the 26th of May, the dire situation Gwyn found himself in, worsened further. The pocket of protection around the beaches was squeezed even further and was on the verge of collapse, when the order was given for all to withdraw to the beach for emergency evacuation. At 0900 hrs. on the 27th, the 175th Bty were ordered to the beach at Zuydcoot, where there were navy ships en route to evacuate them by midnight. However, 30 minutes from their destination, the battery was attacked by low-flying enemy aircraft, forcing them to find cover. Lt-Col Tortise advanced to Zuydcoot by car to halt the deportation of the rescue vessels as it would be impossible for his men to make it by midnight. Upon his arrival, he reported the beach was 'thronged', with Allied troops and there was no staff organisation apparent. This chaos was caused partly as those on the beach were unable to make further contact with the navy and therefore had no ships offshore onto which they could escape.

At 0230 hrs. Gwyn's 175th bty had made it to the beach at Zuydcoot in the hope that Lt-Col Tortise had been successful in halting the Navy, only to discover the same chaos that the Lt-Col had earlier. The second the bemused men stepped foot on the beach, they were dispersed into the nearby dunes of Zuydcoot. Here, they found cover from the Luftwaffe whilst they attempted to contact the navy. After successfully reaching the admirals who were orchestrating the evacuation, Gwyn's superiors were informed of the miscommunication that had caused the confusion. The rescue ships would be arriving at dawn, not midnight, and therefore they should be ready for embarkation in the early hours of the morning.

Under Siege

As the night settled over Dunkirk, the beaches became a battleground. The relentless drone of German aircraft overhead signalled the start of a long and harrowing night. Gwyn and his comrades, huddled together on the sand, bracing themselves for the onslaught. The Luftwaffe's bombing runs had one objective: to obliterate any hope of escape.

The distant thud of explosions sent shockwaves through the makeshift camp. Flares lit up the sky like malevolent fireworks, revealing the chaotic scene below. The Germans were determined to disrupt the evacuation at any cost.

As bombs fell perilously close, Gwyn and his fellow soldiers sought whatever cover they could find. The beach offered little protection, and the sense of vulnerability was overwhelming. Each explosion sent showers of sand and debris cascading over them, a constant reminder of the perilous reality they faced.

Gwyn's ears rang with the cacophony of war, the whine of diving Stukas, the thunderous blasts of explosions, and the staccato of machine gun fire. The sand beneath his fingers felt gritty and unforgiving as he dug trenches with his comrades to provide some measure of shelter. The night air was thick with the acrid scent of burning oil and the sharp tang of cordite.

Amidst the chaos, Gwyn saw flashes of heroism. His fellow soldiers displayed unwavering courage, tending to the wounded and comforting those in distress. The camaraderie that had developed over weeks of service now manifested in acts of selflessness and solidarity. Gwyn knew that their survival depended not only on their individual resolve but on their collective strength.

The darkness seemed endless, punctuated only by the eerie glow of fires on the horizon. Gwyn's thoughts turned to his family back in Wales, and he silently prayed that he would have the chance to see them again. The weight of responsibility bore heavily on his shoulders as he helped maintain a perimeter, scanning the skies for enemy planes.

Despite the relentless assault, Gwyn and his comrades held their ground. They knew that the fate of thousands hung in the balance, and their determination to survive and protect one another was unwavering. As the night wore on, they clung to the hope that dawn would bring a reprieve and the long-awaited rescue they so desperately needed.

The hours felt like an eternity, but with the first light of dawn, a glimmer of hope appeared on the horizon. The Luftwaffe's attacks began to wane, and the distant rumble of artillery fire retreated. Gwyn and his comrades, weary and battle-worn, had weathered the storm. The Dunkirk beaches, though scarred and battered, still held the promise of escape.

At 0400 hrs. on the 28th, one destroyer and two smaller ships appeared offshore. This filled Gwyn with mixed feelings. The elation of finally seeing a small glimmer of safety, but on the other hand, he was all too aware that those vessels alone would not be able to provide rescue for even a fraction of the men desperate to escape that beach. His concerns were validated when these three vessels departed with only 300 troops having been evacuated. Filled with anger and the disappointment of having safety teased under his nose, at 0530 hrs. Gwyn was ordered to find cover in the dunes until further vessels arrived. Hours passed while he sheltered in the sand, praying each shot and explosion wasn't directed towards him. News of further ships being sent finally arrived at 1630 hrs. however, it took until 2100 hrs. for the twelve destroyers to finally appear.

The palpable excitement rippled through the dunes as each man hoped this would be their opportunity for rescue. Evacuation began immediately but proved slow and difficult as only small whalers and rowing boats were able to make it to the shore.

Having endured all the danger they wished to, at 2200 hrs. the twelve destroyers departed for Britain having only rescued 3500 troops. Filled again with disappointment, the troops were ordered to find cover for the night.

The night brought with it a haunting silence, broken only by the distant sound of gunfire and the occasional drone of aircraft. Gwyn and his comrades huddled together for warmth, sharing stories of their journey and dreams of the future. In the darkness, the Dunkirk beaches became a place of shared hope and collective resilience, where the echoes of their courage would resonate through history.

Much like the previous day, the early sunlight broke on the 29th, bringing with it a fresh opportunity for escape. As Gwyn awaited his turn to board an evacuation vessel, the air resonated with the distant rumble of explosions and the overhead drone of aircraft. The perilous nature of their situation was palpable, each passing minute laden with the uncertainty of survival. The evacuation, while a lifeline for those stranded, was also a perilous endeavour, with the threat of air raids casting a dark shadow over the operation.

0500 hrs. on the 29th saw a collection of crafts of all

shapes and sizes appear on the horizon. The evacuation vessels, ranging from naval destroyers to civilian fishing boats, formed an eclectic fleet united by a singular mission – to ferry the stranded soldiers across the English Channel to safety. Gwyn, surrounded by his comrades, marvelled at the makeshift armada that had assembled to defy the perils of Dunkirk. The civilian vessels, manned by everyday heroes, became symbols of courage in the face of overwhelming adversity.

As Gwyn gathered alongside the other desperate troops along the beach in the hope that finally they would be permitted to board one of these vessels, he noticed the weather turning for the worse. The wind whipped up dramatically causing the breaking tide to pound the shore. The smaller vessels that waited patiently offshore swayed violently in the rough sea as the powerful waves washed over the deck. An issue became evident as a lone rowing boat appeared perilously floating towards the shore. On it was a naval officer who insisted the breakers were far too harsh to safely evacuate men from the beach. He therefore recommended to those in charge that they order the men to make their way to Dunkirk immediately, where they could be evacuated via the Jetty. It was a recommendation that was accepted immediately, and Instructions were given for all to make their way by foot, along the battle-scarred beach, to Dunkirk.

Escape

As he arrived at Dunkirk, Gwyn found himself amidst a sea of soldiers, their faces etched with a mixture of exhaustion, anticipation, and fear. The sight of the crowded beaches was overwhelming. The vast expanse of sand stretched out before him, dotted with soldiers and destroyed equipment, all waiting for their turn to escape the looming threat of the German forces. The salty sea breeze mingled with the acrid smell of burning fuel, creating an eerie atmosphere. The Dunkirk beaches, once a picturesque retreat, had transformed into a place of desperation and determination.

Gwyn's mind raced with thoughts of home, of his family waiting anxiously for news of his safety. The uncertainty weighed heavily on him, but he knew that his duty was to stay resolute and await his turn. As the sun rose from the horizon, casting long shadows on the beach, Gwyn couldn't help but wonder if he would make it out of Dunkirk alive.

His unit, the 175th Bty, moved forward in a tense and orderly fashion, following the commands of their officers. The air was thick with tension, punctuated by the distant rumble of artillery fire. The Luftwaffe's menacing presence overhead was a constant reminder that danger lurked just beyond the horizon. Gwyn and his comrades knew that every moment counted; the enemy was closing in, and they had to evacuate swiftly. The evacuation process was a surreal mix of chaos and coordination. Soldiers from various units converged on the beaches, creating a patchwork of uniforms and accents. Gwyn's footsteps left imprints on the sandy shore, a tangible mark of his presence in this historic moment. He glanced at the faces of his fellow soldiers, some of whom he had come to know like brothers during their shared journey through France and Belgium.

The hours passed by in a blur as Gwyn and his comrades waited their turn to board the waiting vessels. They watched as ships of all sizes, from destroyers to civilian fishing boats, arrived to ferry the stranded troops to safety. The line of men waiting to embark seemed endless, a testament to the sheer scale of the operation.

The Naval Rescue

Gwyn and his comrades watched with a mixture of

relief and apprehension as they prepared to board one of the waiting ships. The arrival of the naval and civilian vessels marked a turning point in their ordeal, but the logistics of the evacuation were still daunting.

Gwyn's unit was directed to board one of the smaller passenger ships. As he stepped onto the deck, the planks creaking beneath his boots, he couldn't help but feel a sense of uncertainty. The vessel was crowded with soldiers, each one carrying the weight of their own experiences and fears.

The SS Tynwald was a passenger ship belonging to the 'Isle of Man Steam Packet Company' and was used primarily between Liverpool and Douglas before she was requisitioned by the navy at the beginning of the war. She made her first trip to Dunkirk on the 28th of May and was one of ten personnel ships that rescued 14760 troops from the eastern mole the following day, with Gwyn amongst them.

The crew of the ship, a mix of naval personnel and civilian volunteers, worked tirelessly to organize the troops. Gwyn watched as they directed soldiers to their positions, ensuring that every available inch of space was utilized. The sense of urgency hung in the air as the crew knew that time was of the essence.

As the vessel pulled away from the shore, Gwyn couldn't help but steal a glance back at Dunkirk. The beaches, now distant, were still shrouded in smoke and chaos. The memory of the relentless bombardment and the camaraderie among soldiers lingered in his mind. He knew that many of his fellow comrades were still waiting for their chance to escape.

At 0730 hrs. on the 29th, as Gwyn's vessel set sail, the sea itself became a battleground. The Luftwaffe, relentless in their pursuit, descended upon the evacuation fleet with a fury that mirrored the desperation of their advance in France. The perils of aerial bombardment, coupled with the treacherous waters of the Channel, heightened the sense of danger and urgency. Gwyn, now a participant in this epic evacuation, felt the weight of the perils and the responsibility to persevere against all odds.

The journey across the English Channel was fraught with tension. German aircraft continued to harass the evacuation, and the threat of attack loomed over the vessel. Gwyn's fingers tightened around his rifle as he scanned the skies, a habit formed during his time on the Dunkirk beaches.

Despite the danger, a sense of unity pervaded the vessel. Soldiers from various units shared stories of their experiences at Dunkirk, forming new bonds amidst the uncertainty. The crew, too, displayed unwavering resolve, their determination to see their fellow countrymen to safety evident in their actions.

As they approached the shores of Britain, Gwyn felt a mixture of relief and gratitude. The Dunkirk evacuation had tested their courage and resolve, and they had emerged from the crucible of war with their lives intact. The sight of the British coastline was a welcome beacon, a symbol of home and safety. The boat docked at Dover, and Gwyn and his comrades disembarked onto British soil. The familiar accents of the naval personnel and the gratitude of the civilians who had volunteered to assist them were heartwarming. Gwyn couldn't help but feel a profound sense of gratitude for their safe passage.

As he looked back at the vessel that had carried them to safety, he knew that the Dunkirk evacuation had been a defining moment in his life. It was a testament to the resilience of the human spirit, the bonds formed in times of crisis, and the enduring legacy of those who had faced the crucible of war and emerged stronger for it.

Safe Passage to Britain

As the boat from Dunkirk docked at Dover, Gwyn Morgan and his comrades disembarked onto British soil with a profound sense of relief. They had escaped the chaos of Dunkirk, but the ordeal had left its mark.

From Dover, Gwyn and his fellow soldiers were directed to proceed to Folkestone. The journey was a mix of exhaustion and anticipation as they boarded the waiting transport vehicles for the short trip. As the vehicles rumbled along the roads, Gwyn couldn't help but reflect on the events that had brought him to this moment.

Folkestone was abuzz with activity, as soldiers from Dunkirk joined others who had arrived earlier. Gwyn and his comrades found themselves in a sea of khaki uniforms, a testament to the scale of the evacuation. The magnitude of the operation was both awe-inspiring and sobering.

The respite in Folkestone was brief, and Gwyn soon found himself boarding yet another truck, this time a much more comfortable one, and embarked upon his Journey bound for an undisclosed location in Britain. The truck was crowded with soldiers from different units huddled together, sharing tales of their experiences at Dunkirk. The sense of camaraderie among these men was palpable. Gwyn's thoughts turned to the Dunkirk beaches, to the comrades who were still waiting for their chance to escape, and to the resilience that had carried them through. The journey in the truck was uneventful, a stark contrast to the perils they had faced just days earlier.

As the truck approached its destination, Gwyn couldn't help but feel a mixture of emotions. The Dunkirk evacuation had been a defining moment in his life, one that had tested his courage and resolve. Now, they had arrived on the shores of Britain once more, it was a chance to regroup and reflect on the challenges that lay ahead.

The vehicle arrived at an undisclosed location, and Gwyn and his comrades piled out, ready to face whatever the future held. They knew that the Dunkirk evacuation had been a pivotal chapter in their wartime experiences, one that had forged bonds of camaraderie and resilience that would stay with them throughout their lives.

As Gwyn looked around at his fellow soldiers, he

couldn't help but feel a deep sense of pride and gratitude. The Dunkirk evacuation had been a testament to the strength of the human spirit and the enduring bonds formed in times of crisis. It was a chapter in his life that he would carry with him, a reminder of the sacrifices and triumphs of those who had faced the crucible of war.

The evacuation, while marked by acts of individual heroism, was also a collective endeavour. Gwyn and his fellow soldiers, alongside civilians who had volunteered their vessels, forged a bond born out of necessity. The shared perils and collective perseverance created a sense of unity among the evacuees, transcending military ranks and societal divisions. In those dire moments, humanity itself became a force capable of withstanding the perils that besieged Dunkirk.

Moments of Humanity

During the relentless bombardment on the Dunkirk beaches, Gwyn bore witness to moments of humanity that transcended the chaos of war. As he and his comrades huddled together for safety, he couldn't help but notice the acts of compassion and bravery that unfolded around him.

Amidst the deafening cacophony of explosions and

the ominous drone of aircraft, Gwyn saw soldiers extending helping hands to their wounded comrades. They administered makeshift first aid with whatever supplies they had, often under the dim light of flares. These acts of selflessness were a testament to the unbreakable bonds formed between soldiers in the crucible of battle.

As the night wore on, Gwyn found himself sharing stories with fellow soldiers, and men from different units and backgrounds. They spoke of their homes, their families, and the dreams they held onto. Amidst the fear and uncertainty, there was a palpable sense of camaraderie—a shared understanding that they were all in this together.

Local civilians, too, played a crucial role in these moments of humanity. Gwyn witnessed Dunkirk's residents braving the danger to offer food and water to the stranded soldiers. These acts of kindness, though simple, were lifelines in a time of crisis. The grateful soldiers accepted these offerings with humility, knowing that the civilians were risking their own safety to provide a measure of comfort.

In one particularly poignant moment, Gwyn watched as a group of soldiers formed a protective circle around a terrified young boy who had become separated from his family. Their reassuring words and gestures provided solace to the frightened child, a stark reminder that even in the face of war, compassion endured.

Acts of heroism were not in short supply either. Gwyn saw men dash into the line of fire to rescue wounded comrades, their bravery shining brightly amidst the darkness of war. These were the moments that left an indelible mark on Gwyn's memory—the unwavering resolve of ordinary individuals pushed to extraordinary lengths.

In the early hours of dawn, as the Luftwaffe's attacks began to wane, Gwyn found himself standing shoulder-to-shoulder with soldiers he had never met before. They exchanged nods of acknowledgement and shared smiles of relief. These were the bonds forged in the crucible of adversity, connections that transcended divisions of rank or nationality.

As daylight broke over the Dunkirk beaches, Gwyn felt a profound sense of gratitude for the moments of humanity he had witnessed. The acts of compassion, camaraderie, and bravery were the threads that wove together the tapestry of Dunkirk's resilience. They were the reminders that, even in the darkest of times, the human spirit could shine brightly.

In the days that followed, Gwyn would carry these moments with him as he boarded a vessel bound for Britain. The Dunkirk evacuation had tested the limits of endurance, but it had also revealed the enduring strength of the human spirit. Gwyn's journey was far from over, but he knew that the moments of humanity he had experienced on those beaches would stay with him, a testament to the unbreakable bonds forged in the crucible of war.

Facing the Abyss

The evacuation from Dunkirk, while a triumph in rescuing a significant number of Allied forces, did not diminish the gravity of the situation. As Gwyn disembarked in Dover, the scars of Dunkirk were etched not only on the physical landscape but on the collective consciousness of those who had faced the abyss of imminent defeat. The beaches of Dunkirk, now devoid of the masses that had sought refuge, told a silent tale of the perilous days and nights that unfolded. The remnants of abandoned equipment, the echoes of gunfire, and the haunting quietude stood as a testament to the thin line between survival and surrender. Gwyn, as he surveyed the scene, felt the weight of the abyss they had narrowly escaped, the precipice that separated hope from despair.

The faces of the evacuated soldiers mirrored the collective ordeal. Fatigued and battle-worn, they bore witness to the horror of war and the perilous journey they had undertaken. The camaraderie forged in the crucible of Dunkirk became a shared acknowledgement of the abyss that had loomed over them, a thought that haunted their every step.

As Gwyn reunited with his fellow soldiers in Folkstone, a sense of relief mingled with the awareness that the reality of war still yawned wide. The strategic withdrawal from Dunkirk, while a feat of logistical brilliance, underscored the harsh reality that the enemy's advance had not been halted. The impending threat, like a relentless tide, continued to advance, and Gwyn and his comrades faced the daunting task of regrouping and preparing for the battles that lay ahead.

The aftermath of Dunkirk brought a sombre reflection on the perils faced and the sacrifices made. Gwyn, amidst the military encampments and the war-weary faces, contemplated the war not only as a physical battleground but as a metaphorical abyss that tested the resilience of the human spirit. The shadows of Dunkirk lingered, a reminder that the war, far from over, demanded unwavering determination and sacrifice.

In the halls of military command, Gwyn and his fellow soldiers received briefings that underscored the gravity of the situation. The horrors of war, though momentarily pushed back by the evacuation, still cast its shadow over the Allied forces, urging them to face the future with unwavering courage.

The civilian population, too, grappled with the uncertainty. The echoes of Dunkirk reverberated through communities as they absorbed the impact of the war's proximity. Gwyn, who had witnessed the resilience of civilians during the evacuation, now recognized the symbiotic relationship between the military and civilian populations in facing the abyss together.

As Gwyn and his comrades underwent reorganization and reinforcement, the war took on a new dimension. The uncertainty of the future, the daunting prospect of prolonged conflict, and the relentless pursuit of victory created an atmosphere that stretched beyond the immediate battlegrounds. Gwyn, now more than ever, felt the weight of responsibility to face the enemy not just as a soldier but as a guardian of the future. Gwyn, with a steely resolve forged in the crucible of Dunkirk, faced the future not with fear but with a commitment to stand firm against the encroaching darkness. The unfolding chapters of the war would determine whether they could navigate the abyss and emerge on the other side, victorious against all odds.

Redemption in Retreat

The retreat from Dunkirk marked a crucible of redemption for Gwyn and his comrades. As they regrouped on English soil, the dread of imminent defeat that had loomed over Dunkirk became a catalyst for redemption, a testament to the resilience and determination that defined their collective spirit.

In the aftermath of the evacuation, Gwyn found himself grappling with conflicting emotions. The retreat, though strategically necessary, carried the weight of leaving behind French and Belgian allies, of witnessing the devastation brought upon the landscapes they had fought to defend. The haunting images of abandoned equipment and the echoes of the last stand at Dunkirk lingered, casting a shadow over the redemption they sought.

The military command, recognizing the valour displayed amidst the chaos of Dunkirk, framed the retreat as a tactical manoeuvre rather than a retreat in defeat. The narrative of redemption emerged, emphasizing the heroic efforts to save a substantial portion of the Allied forces. Gwyn and his fellow soldiers. once burdened by the prospect of failure, now saw Dunkirk as a redemptive chapter in the face of overwhelming odds.

Gwyn, as he interacted with the resilient communities that had opened their homes and hearts to the evacuated soldiers, witnessed the redemption not just in military manoeuvres but in the unity of purpose shared by soldiers and civilians alike. They were not discarded for the loss they had encountered but respected for the miraculous escape they had been a part of.

As Gwyn and his unit underwent intensive training and preparation for the battles that lay ahead, the redemption they sought became a beacon of hope. The scars of Dunkirk, instead of being marks of defeat, became symbols of resilience. The redemption in retreat was not merely a tactical manoeuvre but a psychological triumph, a reaffirmation that the spirit of the Allied forces could withstand the darkest moments of the war.

The Aftermath

The aftermath of Dunkirk reverberated across the English Channel, leaving an indelible mark on Gwyn and his fellow soldiers. The evacuation, though hailed as a miraculous rescue, cast a long shadow of contemplation and assessment. As the dust settled and the echoes of conflict subsided, Gwyn found himself amidst the aftermath, a landscape shaped by the trials of retreat and the looming spectre of continued war.

The beaches of Dunkirk, once a chaotic theatre of evacuation, now bore the scars of the harrowing days. Abandoned equipment, remnants of makeshift defences, and the litter of war created a surreal picture. In the wake of the evacuation, Gwyn's unit faced a dual challenge – recovering from the physical and emotional toll of Dunkirk while preparing for the relentless battles that lay ahead. The aftermath was a time of reorganization, assessing losses and reinforcing the ranks. The scars, both visible and hidden, served as reminders of the price paid for each step back from the advancing enemy.

The civilian vessels that had played a pivotal role in

the evacuation now returned to their usual pursuits, leaving the beaches of Dunkirk to reclaim a semblance of normality.

The saved troops, though a fraction of the overall Allied forces, represented a nucleus of resistance. Gwyn, as he underwent debriefings and strategic discussions, realized that the aftermath was not just a moment of reflection but a prelude to a protracted conflict that would shape the destiny of nations.

As the news of Dunkirk reached the home front, the aftermath unfolded in living rooms and town squares. Families waited anxiously for any word of their loved ones who had been part of the evacuation. The aftermath, seen through the lens of those waiting for news, was a tapestry of uncertainty and hope, a delicate balance between despair and the flickering flame of optimism.

Gwyn's own reflections in the aftermath were a mosaic of emotions. The battles fought and the lives lost at Dunkirk became poignant memories. The aftermath, rather than a conclusion, was a continuation of the journey – a journey that now carried the weight of Dunkirk's legacy. Gwyn, as he stood on English soil once more, felt the responsibility that the aftermath imposed – the responsibility to press forward, to honour the sacrifices made, and to ensure that Dunkirk's lessons were not in vain.

The aftermath, as Gwyn would come to realize, was not a static state but a dynamic phase in the evolution of war. It was a period of regrouping, reassessment, and readiness for the next chapter. The aftermath demanded resilience and determination, qualities that Gwyn and his fellow soldiers had homed in the crucible of Dunkirk.

As the military command strategized and the soldiers prepared for the next phase, the aftermath served as a crucible for leadership. Gwyn, who had emerged from Dunkirk with newfound insights and a sense of purpose, found himself assuming roles of responsibility. The aftermath, with its inherent challenges, became a platform for leaders to emerge and guide their units through the uncertain terrain of war.

CHAPTER EIGHT

A Hero's Return

Gwyn's return to Britain after the harrowing Dunkirk evacuation was a journey filled with contrasting emotions. As he disembarked from the transport vessel onto British soil, he couldn't help but feel a mix of profound relief and lingering trauma. The sight of his homeland, its familiar shores and welcoming faces, was a poignant reminder that he had made it out of the crucible of war alive.

The docks were abuzz with activity, as crowds of well-wishers gathered to greet the returning soldiers. The air was electric with cheers, applause, and heartfelt thanks. Gwyn and his comrades were hailed as heroes, their courage in the face of adversity celebrated by a grateful nation. The hero's welcome was a stark contrast to the chaos and uncertainty they had left behind on the beaches of Dunkirk.

For Gwyn, the homecoming was both a blessing and a burden. As he made his way through the throngs of cheering spectators, he couldn't shake the haunting memories of Dunkirk. The faces of friends and comrades lost in the maelstrom of war haunted his thoughts, a constant reminder of the sacrifices made.

The hero's welcome was tinged with the bitter taste of loss. The public's reaction to the returning soldiers was overwhelming. Gwyn and his comrades were showered with gratitude, admiration, and expressions of profound respect. Strangers approached with handshakes and pats on the back, offering words of heartfelt thanks. It was a reminder that the sacrifices made on the beaches of Dunkirk had not gone unnoticed or unappreciated.

As Gwyn looked around at the cheering crowds, he

couldn't help but feel a profound sense of humility. He was just one of many who had faced the crucible of war, and the hero's welcome was a testament to the collective strength and resilience of the British people. Their unwavering support was a source of solace and encouragement, a reminder of the importance of the work he and his fellow soldiers had undertaken.

The hero's welcome touched Gwyn's heart and fueled his determination to continue serving his country. It was a solemn promise to the comrades he had lost and the countless others who had faced the horrors of war. Gwyn knew that the journey was far from over, but he also knew that the hero's welcome had rekindled the flame of resolve in his heart.

As he stood on British soil, looking out at the sea that had brought him home, Gwyn couldn't help but reflect on the remarkable journey he had undertaken. The hero's welcome was a chapter in his life that he would carry with him, a reminder of the enduring spirit of those who had faced the crucible of war and emerged stronger for it.

Physical and Psychological Recovery

After the tumultuous journey of Dunkirk, Gwyn found himself on British soil, his body and mind bearing the scars of war. The hero's welcome was heartwarming, but it was also a stark reminder of the sacrifices made and the comrades lost. In the days that followed his return, Gwyn began the arduous process of physical and psychological recovery.

Physically, Gwyn's body bore the marks of the Dunkirk evacuation. His fatigue was palpable, his muscles sore from days of relentless tension and exertion. The scars from minor wounds and scratches were a testament to the dangers faced on the beaches. It was a reminder that even heroes were not immune to the harsh realities of war.

The process of physical recovery was gradual but steady. Gwyn and his fellow soldiers received medical attention; their wounds were tended to by dedicated healthcare professionals. The nourishing meals provided by the military helped replenish their strength, and the rest they had longed for on the beaches became a cherished reality.

Psychologically, the return to Britain was a journey

through the labyrinth of emotions. The memories of Dunkirk, both the acts of heroism and the loss of friends, weighed heavily on Gwyn's mind. The trauma of war had left an indelible mark, one that would shape his thoughts and actions for years to come.

In the quiet moments of reflection, Gwyn grappled with the questions that haunted him. He wondered why he had been spared when others had not been so fortunate. The guilt of survival gnawed at him, a burden that he carried in silence. He knew that the psychological scars of war were not easily healed.

During this time, Gwyn found solace in the camaraderie of his fellow soldiers. They shared their stories, their fears, and their hopes for the future. The bonds formed on the beaches of Dunkirk grew stronger as they supported one another through the process of recovery. It was in these moments of vulnerability that Gwyn realized he was not alone in his struggle.

As the days turned into weeks, Gwyn's physical strength returned, and his psychological wounds began to heal, albeit slowly. He knew that the process of recovery was ongoing, that the echoes of Dunkirk would linger in his memory. But he was determined to honour the memory of his comrades and the sacrifices made by continuing to serve his country.

Gwyn's journey of recovery was a testament to the resilience of the human spirit. It was a reminder that even in the darkest of times, there was a glimmer of hope, a spark of determination that could overcome the trauma of war. As he looked ahead to the challenges that lay in store, Gwyn knew that he carried with him the lessons learned on the beaches of Dunkirk—the strength to endure and the courage to continue.

Rearming in Aberystwyth

After the hero's welcome back in Britain, Gwyn Morgan and his unit found themselves on a new assignment—to rearm and prepare for the next phase of their service. They were directed to Aberystwyth, a picturesque coastal town on the west coast of Wales. For Gwyn, the journey to Aberystwyth held a sense of anticipation, as well as a deep desire to continue serving his country.

The town of Aberystwyth was a stark contrast to the war-torn landscapes he had recently left behind. Its idyllic coastal setting, with rolling hills and serene beaches, offered a respite from the chaos of war. Yet, Gwyn and his comrades knew that their time here would be far from leisurely. They were on a mission to rearm and prepare for whatever challenges lay ahead.

Their arrival in Aberystwyth marked the beginning of a process of rebuilding and retraining. The unit's weapons and ammunition had been expended during the Dunkirk evacuation, and it was crucial to replenish their supplies. Gwyn and his fellow soldiers were tasked with the meticulous job of inspecting and cleaning newly issued weapons, ensuring they were ready for action.

The training grounds of Aberystwyth became a place of both physical exertion and mental preparation. Gwyn and his comrades honed their marksmanship skills, conducted drills, and simulated combat scenarios. The routine was rigorous, a reminder that the war was far from over and that they needed to be in peak condition to face the challenges ahead.

As the days turned into weeks, Gwyn found himself reflecting on the war so far. The loss of friends and comrades at Dunkirk weighed heavily on his mind. He knew that the crucible of war had changed him, and forged him into a soldier with a deeper understanding of sacrifice and duty. The determination to honour the memory of those who had fallen fueled his resolve.

Aberystwyth, with its serene coastal beauty, offered moments of respite amidst the training and preparation. Gwyn would steal moments to walk along the beach, gazing out at the vastness of the sea. The sound of the waves crashing against the shore was a reminder of the enduring spirit of the British people and the ever-constant ebb and flow of life.

The anticipation of being redeployed loomed on the horizon. Gwyn and his unit knew that their next assignment could take them anywhere, to face new challenges and unknown adversaries. The sense of duty and the bonds forged in the crucible of war kept them resolute, ready to answer the call when it came.

As Gwyn looked out at the sea from the coastal town of Aberystwyth, he couldn't help but feel a profound sense of purpose. The journey was far from over, and the war would demand more from him and his comrades. They had rearmed, both in terms of weapons and spirit and were prepared to face whatever lay ahead in defence of their homeland.

Defending Gloucester

Gwyn Morgan's journey through wartime Britain led him to a new chapter in his service—the defence of the 'Gloucester Aircraft Company.' As he and his comrades arrived in Gloucester, they were acutely aware of the strategic importance of their mission. The aircraft company represented not only a vital industrial asset but also a symbol of British resilience in the face of adversity.

The move to Gloucester brought a new sense of purpose for Gwyn and his fellow soldiers. Their role was clear—to protect the 'Gloucester Aircraft Company' from potential aerial attacks by the enemy. The anticipation of the task ahead was met with a determination to defend this critical piece of the war effort.

The setting was unlike anything Gwyn had experienced before. The sprawling facility was a testament to British ingenuity and industry, with hangars housing aircraft in various stages of production. Gwyn marvelled at the scale of the operation and the dedication of the workers who kept the factory running even in the midst of war.

Gwyn's unit was tasked with patrolling the perimeter of the aircraft company, ensuring its safety day and night. As he walked the grounds, he couldn't help but feel a sense of responsibility weighing heavily on his shoulders. The aircraft company represented more than just machinery; it was a symbol of hope and resilience for the British people.

The days in Gloucester were filled with a sense of alertness and readiness. Gwyn and his comrades maintained constant vigilance, scanning the skies for any sign of enemy aircraft. The threat of attack was ever-present, and the importance of their mission weighed on their minds.

The camaraderie among the soldiers deepened as they faced this new challenge together. They shared stories, played cards during downtime, and found solace in the companionship of their fellow soldiers. The bonds formed in the crucible of war were unbreakable, and Gwyn knew that he could rely on his comrades in the darkest of times.

Life in Gloucester, though defined by the ever-present threat of attack, had its moments of normality. Gwyn and his comrades would often find respite in the nearby town, where they mingled with the locals and experienced moments of warmth and hospitality. These brief interludes provided a glimpse of the resilience of the British spirit.

As the weeks turned into months, Gwyn and his unit continued their vigilance, ensuring the safety of the 'Gloucester Aircraft Company.' The relentless determination to protect this symbol of British resolve became a driving force in their lives. They knew that their mission was not only about defending a factory but also safeguarding the dreams and aspirations of their fellow countrymen.

Gwyn's time in Gloucester was marked by the unyielding commitment to his duty and the bonds formed with his fellow soldiers. The defence of the 'Gloucester Aircraft Company' was a chapter in his wartime journey that would shape his view of the war and the enduring spirit of the British people.

Life Between Alarms

Amid the backdrop of wartime chaos, Gwyn's day-to-day life in Gloucester assumed a rhythm of its own. The days began early, often with the piercing wail of the air raid siren serving as his alarm clock.

Each morning, he would spring into action, donning his uniform and grabbing his helmet, ready to take shelter at a moment's notice.

The city of Gloucester had taken on an air of grim determination. The streets were lined with sandbags, and the facades of buildings were darkened to reduce the risk of bombing raids. Yet, life went on. Gwyn and his comrades patrolled the city's streets, maintaining constant vigilance. They would exchange nods and quick greetings with locals, a shared understanding of the gravity of their situation binding them together.

In the evenings, when the all-clear siren sounded, Gwyn and his friends would often gather at a local pub, the "Red Lion," a refuge of sorts from the daily tension. There, they would unwind, sharing stories and laughter as they tried to forget if only briefly, the shadows that loomed overhead.

As the weeks turned into months, Gwyn's duties took him to various parts of Gloucester. He became intimately familiar with the city's layout, from its bustling docks along the river Severn to the narrow streets of the historic centre. He patrolled the perimeter of the Gloucester Aircraft Company, standing guard with a watchful eye as the workers inside toiled to produce aircraft for the war effort.

As the seasons changed, so did Gwyn's experiences. The winter brought bitterly cold nights spent in cramped air raid shelters, where the camaraderie among the shelter's occupants was a source of warmth in itself. Spring brought renewed hope as the Allied forces made gains on multiple fronts, sparking a glimmer of optimism among the residents of Gloucester.

Through it all, Gwyn forged enduring friendships with his fellow soldiers. Their shared experiences, from the tension of air raids to the mundane moments of downtime, bound them together in a way that transcended the rigours of military service.

Life between alarms was a delicate balance, a tightrope walk between duty and humanity. Gwyn's time in Gloucester revealed not only the resilience of the human spirit but also the strength of the bonds he had formed with his comrades. It was in those moments, amidst the sirens and uncertainty, that he found the resolve to carry on, fueled by the enduring spirit of a nation at war.

CHAPTER NINE

Transfer to Kent

The journey from Gloucester to Kent was a transition that left an indelible mark on Gwyn. The verdant countryside of Kent stretched out before him, a stark contrast to the urban landscape he had grown accustomed to. The decision to move their anti-aircraft regiment to this strategic location was clear – Kent's proximity to London made it a crucial position for the regiment HQ where its batteries would be scattered throughout the area south of the Thames estuary. As Gwyn and his comrades settled into their new surroundings, they found themselves stationed in a quaint corner of the county.

The county of Kent, with its picturesque streets and friendly locals, offered a stark contrast to the war-torn cities they had left behind. It was a welcome respite from the constant tension, a place where they could momentarily escape the shadows of war.

Their battery HQ was positioned at the northern edge of Kent in the small industrial town of Northfleet, west of Gravesend. The 175th battery's gun site was around 8 miles to the southeast in Strood that sat on the border with Essex. The site overlooked the vast expanse of buildings and water of the river Medway that stretched toward the horizon. From their vantage point, they had a clear view of the night sky, which would soon become a canvas for the fiery trails of anti-aircraft shells.

The routines of military life quickly resumed. Mornings began with roll call, followed by drills and maintenance of their anti-aircraft guns. Gwyn and his comrades grew accustomed to the sights and sounds of their new home – the clatter of boots on cobblestone streets, the scent of fresh Kentish air, and the warmth of local smiles.

Yet, the tranquillity of Strood was often shattered by the piercing wail of air raid sirens. It served as a chilling reminder that they were stationed in the frontline of defence against the relentless German Luftwaffe. When the sirens blared, Gwyn and his unit would spring into action, donning their helmets and taking their positions with a sense of duty that had become second nature.

The people of Kent were quick to embrace the soldiers who had come to defend their towns and, by extension, the entire nation. Local pubs and eateries welcomed the troops, offering a taste of Kent's culinary delights and a fleeting sense of normality. The camaraderie between the soldiers and the townspeople was heartening, a testament to the unbreakable spirit of wartime Britain.

As the days turned into weeks, Gwyn explored the surrounding Kentish countryside during moments of respite. He would walk along the country lanes, passing by quaint cottages and fields of ripening crops. It was a stark contrast to the grim realities of the war, a reminder of the beauty that still existed amidst the chaos.

The transfer to Kent was a chapter in Gwyn's wartime journey that brought both the tranquillity of rural England and the ever-present spectre of conflict. It was here that he and his comrades would stand as a shield against the dark clouds of war gathering on the horizon.

The Blitz Begins

As the first ominous wails of the air raid sirens pierced the night, Gwyn and his comrades in Kent knew that their lives were about to change forever. The Blitz had begun, and they were at the forefront of the defence against the relentless German air raids. It was a nightly struggle against the darkness, fear, and an enemy that sought to break the spirit of London.

Gwyn's role in the anti-aircraft crew became a constant, nerve-wracking routine. Each night, they loaded shells into the massive guns, their steel frames illuminated by the eerie glow of the searchlights. The targets were the roaring bombers flying overhead, their menacing shapes blotting out the stars.

The intensity of the nightly bombings was relentless. The thunderous roar of exploding bombs mixed with the deafening cacophony of anti-aircraft fire created an overwhelming symphony of destruction. Gwyn and his fellow soldiers operated like a well-oiled machine, their lives dependent on their training and teamwork.

Their location in Kent offered a strategic advantage. From this vantage point, they had a clear view of the night sky over the county. Their anti-aircraft battery was part of a network of defences that stretched across the periphery of London, forming a protective barrier against the Luftwaffe's onslaught.

But it was no easy task. The enemy bombers came in waves, their formations ominous and relentless. Gwyn's unit fired volley after volley of shells, trying to hit the moving targets with precision. The constant stress and fatigue weighed heavily on them, but their determination remained unbroken.

In the midst of the chaos, Gwyn often found himself reflecting on the irony of war. The same starry skies that had once filled his heart with wonder were now a backdrop to destruction. The city lights that had once guided him home now beckoned death and destruction.

Despite the fear that gripped him each night, Gwyn's resolve remained steadfast. He knew that their efforts were crucial in protecting not only the city but the entire nation. The bond that formed among the anti-aircraft crews was unbreakable. In the darkest hours, they relied on each other for support, finding strength in their shared purpose.

The Blitz had begun, and Gwyn was a witness to its devastation and heroism. Each night, he and his comrades braved the storm of bombs and fire, standing as London's shield against the relentless enemy. It was a chapter in their lives that would test their mettle and leave an indelible mark on their souls.

A Night to Remember

As December 29th 1940 dawned, Gwyn and his comrades near the capital, had no inkling of the chaos that would soon descend upon London. The air was chilly, and a sense of anticipation hung in the atmosphere, as they went about their duties, preparing for another night of defending the capital.

The eerie wail of the air raid sirens pierced the tranquillity of the evening, signalling the impending danger. Gwyn and his fellow anti-aircraft gunners swiftly took their positions, their faces masked by a combination of determination and trepidation. It was a night that would test their mettle in ways they couldn't have imagined.

As a wave of 136 German bombers approached, the night sky lit up with the fiery trails of falling incendiary bombs. The cacophony of explosions drowned out all other sounds, and the city of London became a raging inferno. The buildings, once familiar landmarks, were reduced to rubble and ashes, their flames illuminating the horror that had befallen them.

Gwyn's role in the maelstrom was nothing short of heroic. Amidst the chaos, he demonstrated unwavering leadership, guiding his crew with precision and courage. They loaded shells into the anti-aircraft guns and aimed at the roaring bombers overhead. The deafening noise was punctuated by the thunderous blasts of exploding shells as they fought to protect their battery and aid the valiant firefighters battling the second great fire of London.

As dawn broke, the once-fiery sky began to reveal the magnitude of the destruction. Gwyn and his comrades stood amidst the ruins, their faces streaked with soot and weariness. It was a night that would forever define their wartime experiences, a night when they had witnessed the full horrors of war and yet emerged as heroes in their own right, but despite their heroism, 160 people died in the attacks, and another 250 were injured.

The memories of that fateful night would stay with Gwyn for the rest of his life. The lines etched on his face, the nightmares that would haunt his sleep—they were the silent reminders of the price paid for defending their homeland. December 29th, 1940, was a night to remember, a night that tested the limits of human courage and compassion in the face of unparalleled devastation.

The Harrowing Raids

In the months that followed, the harrowing raids on London continued. May 1941 brought a series of relentless attacks that further strained the defenders' resolve. Gwyn and his unit faced continuous challenges, from ammunition shortages to the toll of witnessing the destruction of the city they were sworn to protect.

As May's chill gave way to spring's full bloom, the skies above London became a battleground once more. The Luftwaffe unleashed a relentless series of bombing raids, targeting factories, residential areas, and iconic landmarks. Gwyn's anti-aircraft battery was in constant action, their guns barking defiance into the night as enemy bombers descended.

One night, while on duty, Gwyn's unit received a direct hit from a high-explosive bomb. The blast was deafening, and shrapnel filled the air. Miraculously, Gwyn and his comrades emerged mostly unscathed, but their equipment and shelter were in ruins. Undeterred, they salvaged what they could and carried on with their mission.

The cityscape had transformed into a sea of ruins. Buildings that had stood for centuries were reduced to rubble, and the once-familiar streets had become treacherous, their paths obstructed by debris. Gwyn often had to navigate through the wreckage, guided by the eerie glow of fires that raged unchecked in the night. Amidst the chaos, Gwyn and his comrades manned their guns, their determination unwavering as they fought to protect this symbol of hope.

Despite the constant danger and the toll it took on their nerves, Gwyn and his fellow soldiers found strength in their camaraderie. Their shared experiences, the moments of levity amidst the horror, and the unwavering sense of duty bound them together like family. They relied on each other for support, a lifeline in a sea of uncertainty.

The psychological toll of the harrowing raids was impossible to ignore. Sleep came in fits and starts, haunted by the spectre of falling bombs and the screams of the wounded. Gwyn often found solace in the quiet moments between the raids, the brief respite when the skies were momentarily clear, and the city could catch its breath.

May 1941 became a crucible of endurance, a testament to the unyielding spirit of those who defended London. Gwyn and his comrades pressed on, knowing that their sacrifices were part of a larger battle for freedom and survival.

Adapting to Extended Conflict

As the bombing campaign dragged on, Gwyn and his fellow soldiers learned to adapt to the extended conflict. The routines of their daily lives evolved, coping mechanisms were honed, and their duties took on new dimensions. The war had become a relentless marathon, and they were determined to see it through to the end.

GWYN – THE LIFE OF AN UNSUNG SOLDIER

Their days began with the blaring of the alarm sirens, a shrill reminder of the nightly onslaught they would face. The crew's coordination had reached a level of seamless precision that allowed them to respond to threats with mechanical efficiency. Gwyn knew every inch of his anti-aircraft gun, and his comrades had become an extended family, bonded by their shared experiences.

In the quiet moments between air raids, life took on a surreal normality. Gwyn found solace in the small things—writing letters to loved ones, reading dog-eared novels shared among the crew, and exchanging stories of home. The camaraderie that had been forged in the crucible of war grew stronger with each passing day.

The air raids often left the city shrouded in darkness and chaos. London's skyline had transformed into a sea of rubble and flames. Yet, Gwyn and his comrades became the beacons of hope in the night. Their relentless fire into the sky was a defiant answer to the enemy overhead, a testament to the unyielding spirit of the defenders.

Amidst the fear and uncertainty, Gwyn found moments of reflection. He pondered the world beyond the barrage of shells and fire. He longed for the serene landscapes of his homeland, the rolling hills of Wales, and the laughter of his family. The war had aged him beyond his years, and his innocence had been replaced with a steely resolve.

The adaptation to extended conflict also saw Gwyn and his fellow soldiers uniquely experiencing the city of London. In the rare daylight hours, they explored the streets, witnessing the scars of war up close. They marvelled at the resilience of Londoners, who carried on their lives with a stoic determination that mirrored their own.

As the seasons changed, so did their circumstances. The bitter cold of winter gave way to the tentative warmth of spring. Yet, the war showed no sign of abating. Gwyn's coping mechanisms became more ingrained, his spirit unwavering. He drew strength from the knowledge that his efforts were part of a larger tapestry, a fight for freedom and survival that extended far beyond the borders of London. Adapting to extended conflict meant not only enduring the physical demands but also navigating the emotional toll. Gwyn and his comrades faced loss, witnessed devastation, and grappled with the haunting memories of the raids. Yet, they pressed on, their determination unbreakable, their sense of duty unwavering.

On The Move Again

By 1942, Nazi Germany's campaign had stretched across the globe and their failure to win air superiority over Britain had seen Hitler abandon his ambitions to invade the British Isles. With the enemy's air power now focused elsewhere, Gwyn's 175th AA battery was stood down from operational duty and was transferred to the 25 Anti-Aircraft Brigade, which was put on the reserves under the command of the War Office.

The relentless Luftwaffe, met with the furious resilience of the Anti-Aircraft command and the heroic pilots of Fighter Command, took huge losses and were unable to continue with the same intensity. The fortification of Britain was a resounding success, and resisting a Nazi invasion meant an Allied force remained in Europe.

On the 8th of January, the 85th HAA regiment was placed on the army troop reserve roster and issued a training plan which they continued with until they were relieved from their duties in the Thames and Midway south area in the May of 1942. It was at this point that Gwyn and his unit were posted to the Bedhampton Training Camp in Havant, Hampshire, where they would continue their training. They spent a few weeks peacefully training on the south coast until the 8th of June when the regiment was recalled from the reserve roster and ordered back into service.

Intelligence reports suggested that another wave of attacks from the Germans was imminent via land, sea and air, and the 175th battery was issued the task of defending the Portsmouth area from aerial attack, whilst guarding the training complex at Bedhampton from any potential ground attacks.

The battery was split up and assigned various tasks, from manning their familiar 3.7-inch AA gun to guarding entrances and exits. Men would patrol the area on foot, and small sections would be dispersed amongst the woodland surrounding the camp to silently survey the ground for any enemy movement. Despite the brisk response, an attack never came, much to the relief of Gwyn and his comrades.

Back on operational duty meant a fresh posting for Gwyn, and on the 14th of June, he was ordered back to Kent to defend Canterbury, Minster

Thanet, Ashford and Folkestone from any potential aerial attacks. With the regiment HQ set up in the familiar port town of Folkestone. Gwyn's return stirred up a complex mix of emotions. His previous visit to the town was one of desperation and relief, and those feelings began to replay themselves in his mind as he wandered the streets. Luckily, only brief periods of Gwyn's time were spent there, as his battery was posted to a gun position in Marsham near Kennington, just north of Ashford. They were allocated lodgings in an old vicarage nearby, which provided a welcomed home for the men, who had spent many nights sleeping on hard ground in the tents and huts that had been hastily provided for them.

Although Gwyn's time in Kennington saw a few isolated enemy aircraft attempting to spring an attack on the unsuspecting capital, the attempts were thwarted by the sharp reactions of those defending it. Much of the 175th battery's time was spent training and honing their skills in anticipation of further conflict, until the 25th of October 1942, when Gwyn and his 175th battery were again placed on the reserve roster and the 85th HAA regiment were relieved of all operational commitments in the southeast. The order for them to mobilise was given on the 26th, which saw them travel by rail to a staging area in Leeds where further instructions would be given.

Only a day after arriving at Leeds, the unit was being considered for further training camps. On the 5th of January 1943, Gwyn was on a train heading north. The journey took 3 days, each one ending at a rest camp in Carlisle and Wishaw before arriving at the final destination.

Despite being relieved from his frontline defensive duties and placed on the reserves at the War Office, Gwyn was not offered the opportunity to rest within the comforts of Min-Yr-Afon, instead, he found himself and his unit arriving at the unfamiliar city of Dundee.

Gwyn saw his days in Scotland filled with light training drills. Based in a camp on the outskirts of Dundee, the fresh Scottish air filled his lungs as he set off on his morning march and late-night simulations. The peaceful landscape became a comfort to Gwyn as the rolling hills and the calm water of the Firth of Tay reminded him of the rural tranquillity of home.

The months of peace spent in Scotland were also used as an opportunity to share tactical information and training methods between regiments. Practice camps would be created throughout Scotland and the north of England. These camps would allow opportunities for various regiments to train side by side with others, sharing valuable information that could prove vital in future conflict. As well as the useful information Gwyn would have absorbed, these camps would also provide opportunities for him to visit cities and landmarks, allowing him to explore new places and experience what else Britain had to offer. The camp locations included the beautiful Isle of Bute off the west coast of Scotland that skirted the Firth of Clyde, Burrow Head at the southwest of Scotland, Carlisle and Cheshire. The regiment eventually settled at Delamere Camp, Northwich in Cheshire on the 12th of March.

CHAPTER TEN

The Ormonde

By the end of March 1943, the atmosphere around the Delamere camp had begun to change. The volume of conversations increased as they grew shorter and took on a more sinister tone. The sense of impending change clung to the air as whispers of a possible move began to circulate. Despite these hushed conversations, nobody, including Gwyn, was prepared for their next mission.

On the 11th of April 1943, orders were sent for the 85th HAA regiment to move to Hartford LMS Station where they would be loaded onto a train bound for a location that remained unknown. As the men huddled within the cramped trucks that trembled towards the station, Gwyn began to realise that this was no ordinary move, and their destination would not be another lighthearted training camp that gave ample opportunity to explore the local towns and mingle with the civilians. Orders were barked within the trucks that there would be no outside communications during the journey. There must be no telephone calls, letters or telegrams sent or received whilst on route to, or at the embarkation port.

The words, 'Embarkation port', grabbed Gwyn's attention. It was the first time he had heard those words since the order to board the Lady of Mann at Southampton in 1940 was given. Waves of dread and fear came rushing back as he looked around at the other men who visibly shared his trepidation. Thoughts of faraway battles played in Gwyn's mind. The stories told by men who fought in the distant lands of Africa, the Pacific and Eastern Europe were lodged in his mind as he considered each place a potential destination.

Later that day, the port of embarkation became clear as their train came to a stop at Clyde. The day was etched in Gwyn's memory as a moment of both significance and uncertainty. The Ormonde, an imposing ship among the KMF.13 convoy, loomed large before him, its massive hull a testament to the monumental journey they were about to undertake. The bustling port of Clyde was alive with activity, as soldiers boarded ships with a mix of pride and apprehension.

The air was filled with a cacophony of voices, as soldiers hurriedly stowed their gear and officers barked orders. It was a scene of organized chaos, a symphony of duty.

The Ormonde, like a steel behemoth, was alive with activity. Troops scurried up gangplanks, and the cargo hold echoed with the clatter of equipment being loaded. Gwyn and his comrades took their positions, shoulder to shoulder, as they prepared to board the ship that would carry them away from the shores of Britain.

Gwyn spent five days aboard the Ormond, just off the coast of Scotland before, finally, on the 16th of April, the rest of the ships that belonged to the convoy had been loaded and were ready to set sail. Gwyn couldn't help but steal one last look at the receding coastline. The cliffs of Britain, a symbol of home and safety, grew smaller on the horizon. The waves, once a distant murmur, now carried them further from Britain and deeper into the unknown.

Life on board the Ormonde quickly settled into a routine. The ship was a world unto itself, and Gwyn found himself navigating its labyrinth of corridors and narrow passageways. The cramped quarters and steel bulkheads were a stark contrast to the open fields of his homeland. Yet, there was a sense of camaraderie among the soldiers, a shared understanding that they were all in this together.

The daily life on board was a symphony of routines. Soldiers conducted drills, maintaining a level of readiness that was as essential as it was repetitive. The ship's mess hall served as a gathering place, where men from different walks of life shared stories, laughter, and meals. Old letters from loved ones back home were cherished, offering a fleeting connection to the world they had left behind.

In the quiet moments, Gwyn often found himself on deck, gazing out at the endless expanse of the sea. The rhythmic sound of the ship slicing through the waves was a soothing backdrop to his thoughts. He reflected on the events that had led him here, the faces of friends and family he had left behind, and the uncertainty of the journey ahead.

As the Ormonde sailed further from Britain, the mixed feelings of leaving home for an unknown future remained. The ship carried them into uncharted waters, but not yet towards North Africa.

The convoy left Scotland and headed west, deep into the Atlantic Ocean before turning south. This was a strategic plan to avoid the German U-boats and disguise their final destination.

Gwyn knew that the coming days would test their mettle in ways they could not yet fathom, but the bonds formed among the soldiers aboard the Ormonde would serve as a source of strength in the trials to come.

Life at Sea

The Ormonde sailed steadily through the vast expanse of the Atlantic Ocean, its destination: North Africa. Gwyn and his comrades settled into the rhythms of life on board the ship, carving out a semblance of routine amidst the unpredictability of wartime travel.

The days began with the blaring of a bugle, announcing the start of another day at sea. Gwyn would rise from his bunk, the cramped quarters offering little privacy but fostering a sense of camaraderie among the soldiers. Morning drills were conducted on the deck, a reminder that they were soldiers first and foremost, even at sea.

The ship became their world, and it was a world of contrasts. Above deck, the vast blue horizon stretched endlessly, a reminder of the uncertainty that lay ahead. Below deck, the air was thick with the scent of sweat, oil, and the musty smell of a thousand men confined to a metal vessel.

The routines were punctuated by moments of recreation. Card games and makeshift competitions provided fleeting distractions from the monotony. Gwyn found solace in these moments, a brief respite from the ever-present tension that hung in the air.

Letters brought with them from home became cherished treasures. They were read and re-read, their words offering a lifeline to the lives they had left behind. Each letter was a reminder of the loved ones waiting for their safe return, a beacon of hope in the midst of uncertainty.

The sea journey was not without its challenges. Storms would roll in, tossing the ship about like a toy in the hands of a child. Seasickness was a constant companion for some, and Gwyn himself battled bouts of nausea during the roughest moments.

Yet, amidst the hardships, there was a sense of unity among the soldiers. They had become a tightly-knit community, bound by a shared purpose and the knowledge that they could rely on one another in times of need. In the darkness of the ship's belly, they would share stories and dreams, finding solace in the company of their fellow soldiers.

As the Ormonde made its way further from Britain, the weather began to change. The biting cold of the Atlantic gave way to milder temperatures as they turned south. The journey became a time of reflection for Gwyn. He often found himself on the deck at night, gazing up at the star-studded sky. The constellations served as a silent reminder that, no matter how far they had travelled, they were still guided by the same stars that had illuminated their journeys back home.

Life at sea was a paradox, a blend of monotony and intensity. It was a time of physical and emotional challenges, but it was also a time of growth and resilience. As the Ormonde continued its voyage towards North Africa, Gwyn and his comrades were unknowingly preparing for the trials that awaited them in the deserts of a distant land.

The Convoy Experience

Life aboard the Ormonde as part of a vast convoy was a unique blend of routine and tension. Gwyn and his comrades had become intimately familiar with the ship's quarters and the daily rhythms of life at sea.

Mornings began with the call to muster, soldiers lining up in neat rows on the deck as they underwent roll call and received their orders for the day. As the Ormonde sailed alongside its fellow convoy ships, Gwyn couldn't help but marvel at the sheer scale of the operation. The convoy stretched as far as the eye could see, a lifeline connecting the Allied forces in Britain to the distant frontlines of North Africa. It was a reminder that they were part of something much larger, a critical cog in the machinery of war.

Days on board the ship were filled with drills and training exercises. Soldiers practised their marksmanship on the deck, honed their first-aid skills, and rehearsed emergency procedures. The routines were meticulous, a constant reminder of the ever-present danger that lurked beneath the waves.

Evenings offered a temporary respite from the daily drills. Gwyn and his friends often gathered on the deck, swapping stories and sharing laughter. These moments of camaraderie served as a lifeline, a reminder of the bonds that held them together in the face of uncertainty.

The convoy experience was not without its moments of heightened tension. Enemy submarines prowled the waters, a constant threat that kept everyone on edge. Gwyn vividly recalled the first time the ship's siren blared, signalling a possible submarine sighting. Panic rippled through the ranks as soldiers rushed to their battle stations, scanning the waves for any signs of danger.

Naval escorts were a reassuring presence, their ships prowling the perimeter of the convoy like vigilant guardians. The sight of their powerful guns and the knowledge that they were there to protect the convoy bolstered the soldiers' spirits. In the dark hours of the night, searchlights crisscrossed the water, casting eerie shadows on the sea's surface.

During the journey, there were moments of genuine fear and trepidation. The ship's crew and soldiers would spot the telltale signs of a submerged U-boat – the periscope breaking the surface or the faint trace of a torpedo wake. Tense hours would pass as depth charges were dropped into the water, the deafening explosions reverberating through the ship's hull.

The suspenseful encounters with enemy submarines added a dramatic edge to the otherwise routine days at sea. These close calls served as stark reminders of the precarious nature of their journey and the constant threat that lay beneath the waves.

As the convoy neared its destination in Algiers, the tension began to ease. The collective sigh of relief was palpable as the soldiers realized they had successfully navigated the treacherous waters of the Atlantic and were now in the calmer waters of the Mediterranean. They were one step closer to their mission in North Africa, a mission that would demand every ounce of their courage and determination.

Arrival in Algiers

The sight of Algiers, with its white-washed buildings nestled against the Mediterranean coastline, was a stark contrast to the familiar landscapes of Britain. As Gwyn and his comrades disembarked from the Ormonde at 1230 hrs. on the 23rd, they were greeted by the dry, desert air and the foreign sounds of the city. It was a moment of profound transition, and the uncertainty of the future weighed heavily on their minds.

Their initial impressions of Algiers were a mix of fascination and wariness. The city's bustling streets were filled with a vibrant mix of cultures, with French, Arab, and indigenous influences all intermingling. The aromatic scent of spices from market stalls wafted through the air, creating a sensory tapestry that was both exotic and intoxicating.

Despite the strong first impression Algiers had made on Gwyn, his time there was brief as he and his unit were sent straight to a reception area at Sidi Moussa, to the south of Algiers where they would be introduced to life in Africa.

As Gwyn and his unit settled into their new

surroundings, their immediate tasks and challenges came into focus. They were part of a rapidly evolving theatre of war, and adaptability was paramount. Their mission was clear: to contribute to the Allied effort in North Africa. The shifting sands of the desert held secrets and challenges that demanded their unwavering attention.

Their first days in Sidi Moussa were a whirlwind of activity. They underwent briefings and orientation, learning about the local terrain and the tactics required for desert warfare. Gwyn marvelled at the stark beauty of the desert landscape, its endless dunes and unrelenting sun a far cry from the green fields of Britain.

The scorching North African sun beat down on them as they toiled, but the sense of purpose and the knowledge that they were contributing to a larger cause buoyed their spirits.

As Gwyn explored the local towns and villages during his off-duty hours, he couldn't help but be struck by the warmth of the local population. Despite the disruptions caused by war, the people of Algeria displayed a remarkable sense of hospitality. They shared stories, traditions, and meals, forging connections that transcended language barriers.

The transition to North Africa was not without its challenges. The climate, with its searing heat during the day and chilling cold at night, required adaptation. Uniforms were adjusted, and strategies were developed to contend with the harsh conditions. Gwyn and his comrades learned to conserve water and seek shelter from the relentless sun, their survival instincts sharpening with each passing day.

As Gwyn and his unit settled into their new roles, they knew that the North African front would test their mettle in ways they had yet to imagine. The shifting sands of Algeria marked the beginning of a new chapter in their wartime journey, one that would demand courage, adaptability, and unwavering resolve.

Adapting to a New Theater of War

The transition from the battlefields of Europe to the arid expanses of North Africa was nothing short of a culture shock for Gwyn and his comrades. The first challenge they faced was the unforgiving climate. The relentless North African sun beat down upon them, and the scorching heat was unlike anything they had experienced before. The British uniforms, designed for the damp and cool European climate, now felt suffocating in the desert.

As they adjusted to the harsh environment, Gwyn and his fellow soldiers quickly learned the importance of rationing water. The desert's thirst was unrelenting, and water became a precious commodity. They carried canteens and camelbacks, carefully measuring each sip to ensure they had enough to endure the long marches and the relentless heat of the day.

The terrain in North Africa presented its own set of challenges. The shifting sands and rocky desert landscape were vastly different from the familiar European battlegrounds. Gwyn's unit had to adapt to the unique conditions, learning how to navigate the dunes, avoid treacherous quicksand, and make use of the natural cover provided by the rugged terrain.

The nature of warfare in North Africa was also distinct from the trench warfare of Europe. Here, battles were marked by fluidity and mobility. Gwyn and his comrades became adept at desert warfare, mastering the tactics of hit-and-run engagements, ambushes, and long-range desert patrols. They learned the art of camouflage and the importance of blending in with the desert to avoid detection by the enemy.

One of the most striking differences was the introduction of new equipment, including specialized desert uniforms, vehicles, and weaponry. Gwyn and his fellow soldiers traded in their standard-issue Lee-Enfield rifles for the renowned Lee-Enfield No. 4 Mk I rifles, specially adapted for the desert campaign. These rifles became Gwyn's constant companion, and he honed his marksmanship skills in the harsh desert environment.

The challenges of adapting to North Africa were not limited to the physical environment. Gwyn and his comrades also had to familiarize themselves with the complexities of desert tribal politics and navigate the cultural intricacies of the region. Interactions with local Bedouin tribes, who often provided invaluable intelligence and support, required diplomacy and cultural sensitivity.

Despite the hardships and adjustments, Gwyn found moments of beauty in the North African desert. The vast, open skies adorned with a tapestry of stars at night provided solace and inspiration. It was a stark reminder that even in the harshest of environments, there was a profound sense of wonder to be discovered.

As the days passed, Gwyn's unit became a well-oiled machine, seamlessly blending into the desert landscape and executing their drills with precision. The camaraderie forged in the crucible of North Africa was unlike anything they had experienced before. They relied on each other not just for survival but also for the courage to face the uncertainties of the desert war.

In the heart of the North African desert, Gwyn and his comrades found the ability to adapt, the determination to overcome, and the unwavering spirit to continue their fight against the Axis forces. It was in this new theatre of war that Gwyn's mettle was truly tested, and he emerged as a soldier transformed by the challenges of North Africa.

CHAPTER ELEVEN

Arriving in North Africa

The moment Gwyn set foot on the sun-soaked soil of Algiers, he knew he was a world away from the green hills and coastal breeze of Pembrokeshire. The Mediterranean sun blazed mercilessly overhead, casting long shadows across the bustling harbour. The air was thick with the scent of spices and the cacophony of foreign tongues. It was a sensory whirlwind that both overwhelmed and intrigued him.

As he disembarked from the ship, Gwyn joined the stream of fellow soldiers, each one carrying the weight of uncertainty on their shoulders. Their destination was a land wholly unlike their homeland, yet duty called. He recalled the discussions on the ship, the anticipation of the unknown. The whispers of seasoned soldiers painted a picture of a harsh desert landscape, where every grain of sand held secrets of battles past.

Gwyn's unit was soon assigned to a temporary camp on the outskirts of Sidi Moussa. The canvas tents provided minimal shelter from the relentless sun and the sand that seemed to find its way into everything. It was here that Gwyn received his first taste of the challenges that lay ahead. He trained relentlessly, drilling under the North African sun, learning the nuances of desert warfare. They adapted their Anti-Aircraft guns to suit the conditions, knowing that the enemy could strike from the skies at any moment.

In those early days, Gwyn found himself navigating a labyrinth of narrow alleyways and bustling markets. He was captivated by the sights and sounds of Algeria and the vibrant tapestry of cultures that filled its streets. The call to prayer echoed through the city, a haunting melody that reminded him of the profound differences between his homeland and this foreign land. Amidst the challenges and cultural adjustments, Gwyn discovered a camaraderie with his fellow soldiers that transcended borders. The diversity of languages and backgrounds served as a reminder that they were part of a global effort, a coalition of nations united against a common foe.

In the days that followed, Gwyn had the opportunity to interact with the local Algerian population. He ventured into the heart of Sidi Moussa where the markets beckoned with their exotic wares. The locals, though initially cautious, welcomed him with curious smiles. Gwyn tasted the flavours of North Africa, shared stories through gestures when language failed, and witnessed the rich tapestry of daily life.

Algeria became more than just a foreign posting; it became a place where Gwyn's understanding of the world expanded. He marvelled at the intricate tile work of the mosques, the bustling souks, and the resilience of the people who called this land home. The desert sun may have been unrelenting, but it could not dim the warmth of the human connections forged amidst its harsh beauty.

In these initial days in North Africa, Gwyn's world had transformed in profound ways. He was no longer the young man from Pembrokeshire, but a soldier on a foreign shore, ready to face the challenges that lay ahead. The echoes of home were distant, replaced by the vibrant and mysterious rhythms of Algeria, a place that would shape his wartime journey in ways he could never have imagined.

Duties and Drills in a New Land

Gwyn's daily routine was punctuated by the piercing cries of their commanding officer, barking orders that sent them into action. The harsh sun beat down upon them as they drilled relentlessly, fine-tuning their skills in desert warfare. The shifting sands beneath their feet became as familiar as the Welsh soil they once knew, and the sweat and exhaustion were constants in their new reality.

The monotony of desert life was broken by the occasional skirmish or engagement with Axis forces. Gwyn's unit faced moments of intense combat, defending their positions against enemy aircraft and ground forces. The vastness of the desert provided both cover and challenges, and each engagement was a test of their training and resolve. Amidst the harsh realities of their duties, Gwyn found moments of respite in the stillness of the desert night.

As time passed, Gwyn's understanding of desert warfare deepened, and he began to appreciate the unique strategies required to prevail in this unforgiving environment. He witnessed the resilience of his fellow soldiers and the unwavering determination to protect their comrades and the vital supply lines that crisscrossed the continent.

In the heart of the desert, Gwyn had transformed from a young recruit into a seasoned soldier. He had embraced the challenges of his new land, mastered the art of desert warfare, and forged unbreakable bonds with his comrades. The vast desert, once intimidating, had become a canvas upon which Gwyn and his unit painted their newfound abilities.

Interactions with Allies and Locals

As Gwyn settled into life in Algeria and embraced the challenges of desert warfare, he found himself in the company of soldiers from diverse Allied nations. The eclectic mix of accents and backgrounds within his unit was a testament to the global scale of the war effort. The barracks buzzed with conversations in various languages, from English and French to Polish and Dutch. Gwyn marvelled at the tapestry of cultures and stories that surrounded him. Each soldier brought a unique perspective to the war, and late-night conversations often revolved around shared experiences and the longing for home.

Gwyn also had the opportunity to work closely with soldiers from the French Foreign Legion. Their units often collaborated on drills in the desert, and the language barrier dissolved as they learned to communicate through actions and shared objectives. The French soldiers shared their insights into desert survival and warfare, teaching Gwyn and his comrades invaluable lessons that would prove crucial in the months to come.

Gwyn's interactions with the local Algerian children were equally memorable. He would often distribute sweets and small gifts, and in return, he received radiant smiles and laughter that transcended language. These simple yet profound moments served as a reminder of the human connections that could be forged in the most unlikely of places.

Challenges and Triumphs

Sidi Moussa presented Gwyn with a series of formidable challenges, both logistical and personal, as he embarked on his desert warfare journey. One of the earliest hurdles was adapting to the unforgiving desert environment. The relentless sun and blistering heat took a toll on the soldiers, and Gwyn vividly remembered the discomfort of sand getting into every crevice of his uniform. The scarcity of resources tested their ingenuity and resourcefulness. Water, in particular, became a precious commodity, and rationing was a daily reality.

The battery recalled one training exercise in particular when their unit became disoriented in a sandstorm. Visibility plummeted, and their compasses proved unreliable in the shifting sands. It was a moment of profound uncertainty and a stark reminder of the unpredictable nature of their environment.

During these challenges, Gwyn faced moments of personal introspection. He grappled with homesickness, longing for the green hills of Pembrokeshire and the familiar faces of loved ones left behind. It was in these solitary moments, under the vast desert sky, that he found solace in the camaraderie of his fellow soldiers and the shared purpose that bound them together.

In the heart of the desert, Gwyn's resolve was tested, but he emerged from each challenge with newfound strength and determination. The desert, once a harsh and unfamiliar land, had become a crucible in which he and his comrades forged unbreakable bonds and honed their skills as soldiers.

Reflections on War and Distance

As the days passed in Sidi Moussa, Gwyn found himself confronted by moments of introspection that the vastness of the desert often inspired. The relentless sun beating down upon the golden sands became a constant reminder of the unforgiving nature of war. It was during these moments of stillness that he began to contemplate the purpose of the war and the distance that separated him from his homeland.

During his time within the desert's isolation, Gwyn's beliefs began to evolve. He had embarked on this journey as a young man filled with patriotism and a sense of duty. However, the war's unrelenting grip had transformed his perspective. He questioned the true cost of conflict, the lives lost, and the profound impact on those who remained. The endless expanse of the desert seemed to mirror the vastness of the world's suffering.

One particularly poignant moment of reflection occurred during a rare respite from their duties. Gwyn and his comrades gathered beneath the desert stars; their voices hushed by the vastness of the night sky. They spoke of the futility of war, the longing for peace, and the hope for a better future. It was a conversation that transcended nationalities and backgrounds, a testament to the universal desire for a world free from conflict.

The isolation of the desert also allowed Gwyn to revisit memories of his childhood in Letterston. He recalled the laughter of his siblings, the stories shared by the hearth, and the simple pleasures of a bygone era. These recollections provided solace in the midst of hardship, a reminder of the enduring bonds that connected him to his roots.

As time passed, Gwyn's perspective on the war shifted from a sense of duty to a longing for peace.

He began to dream of a world where the echoes of battle were replaced by the sounds of children's laughter and the embrace of loved ones. The distance from home had transformed into a yearning for the familiar comforts of Pembrokeshire.

In the heat of Algeria, under the expansive desert sky, Gwyn's reflections on war and distance became a crucible of transformation. He had evolved from a young recruit into a soldier with a deeper understanding of the human cost of conflict. The desert had become not just a battleground but a place of self-discovery and growth, where he grappled with the profound questions that war had laid before him.

CHAPTER TWELVE

Progress in Northern Africa

Gwyn's time in the Algiers region, although brief, was filled with an endless flurry of activity. That was a carefully designed plan, orchestrated by his commanders to quickly bring his unit up to the standards required to survive the desert.

Gwyn and his fellow soldier's arrival in Algeria was a whirlwind of training and instruction. They mistakenly believed that they were deep in the toughest period of their service. The relentless pressure of drills and maintenance in the searing heat, all while under the constant threat of aerial attack was a momentous task. But as Gwyn soon discovered, this was merely a warmup for the real test that Africa had lined up for him. This period was but a training exercise for what they were to face next.

The challenge of finding their feet in a place so alien to anything that resembled home was a huge one. But it was one that Gwyn and his fellow soldiers embraced by submerging themselves in the local culture. Their willingness to listen and learn from those with knowledge and experience of the area was what allowed them to feel any form of acceptance.

In 1943, as Gwyn's unit were quickly moulded into desert soldiers, other Allied ground forces were making their final push into Tunis, the last Axis stronghold in Northern Africa. The enormous importance of this task weighed heavily on everyone, including those in the relative safety of Sidi Moussa. Taking Tunis would cause the collapse of Rommel's African forces, giving the Allies the ability to strike into the European continent from the south. That though, would only be possible if the ports and harbours along the North African coast could be defended against the Axis aircraft.

Bound for Bone

On the 6th of May 1943, orders were made for Gwyn and his unit to move. Whispers amongst the troops grew louder as some believed they were heading back to northern Europe, while others remained sceptical. But as a whole, the mood was one of optimism. This small glimmer of hope however was short-lived, as they arrived at a staging camp at Beni Mansour, the collective sigh of the disheartened troops was clear. Gwyn, who had remained sceptical of the hope that had lingered within his unit, knew all too well that staging areas were usually a sign that combat would soon follow.

Their unknown destination acted as a barrier which Gwyn could not see past. Yet again, the uncertainty of what was to come attacked his every thought, until he was informed of plans to post the unit to Bone.

The days that followed saw the 85th HAA regiment travel by road across Northern Africa. Firstly, to Ain M'Lila on the 7th and then onwards to Bone on the 8th.

Bone, or Annaba, as it is known today, sits on the northeast coast of Algeria, close to the Tunisian border. With the Allied ground forces battling fiercely in Tunisia, the importance of defending Bone was vital. The small harbour town of Bone, sitting in a position of strategic importance, was the closest port that the Allies were able to hold near the city of Tunis. The importance of defending the harbour was underlined by the arrival of Gwyn and his 175th Bty. Their battle-hardened experience and ability to adapt and overcome obstacles was what brought them to Bone.

Although all of the individual elements suggested this new landscape should be identical to the one Gwyn had become so familiar with in Sidi Moussa, there was something in the air that differed. The atmosphere was thick with trepidation. The nervy faces that raced around, each fixed on their individual tasks, seemed to have no interest in absorbing any unessential information. They were driven by the desire to complete each order they had been given, with their concentration unbreakable.

The prime location of Bone was an asset to the Allied ground forces, as it gave them the ability to import ammunition, equipment, and supplies to Tunisia via the sea, rather than the slower route through the harbour at Algiers and across the land, the route that Gwyn had recently navigated. However, the convenient location of the town also caused problems for the Allies. With the island of Sicily sitting just across the Mediterranean to the east, a hub of Axis aircraft operated out of the city of Catania's airfield. The short 30-minute flight across the Mediterranean meant Bone was a target of high priority for the German and Italian air forces as they attempted to cut off supply routes to the front line at Tunis.

Bone had its own small, makeshift airfield where a few aircraft would scramble to intercept the onslaught of enemy raids, but they were little more than an annoyance to the Axis air forces and most of the defence was left the the Anti-Aircraft units.

Desert Defence

With Gwyn and his finely tuned team of gunners in their position overlooking the hustle of the harbour, their African challenge became a canvas upon which the defenders of Bone would have their names painted.

Their arrival at Bone was marked by their first wave of Luftwaffe attacks only 24 hours after their arrival. 1950 hrs. on the 9th of May saw a swarm of enemy aircraft approaching from the Northeast. As they crossed the Mediterranean they would disperse into streams of unpredictability. Each individually attacked from a different direction causing chaos for the gunners to line up their colossal turrets.

This welcome to Bone saw Gwyn and his battery desperately defending the harbour from the 18 aircraft that attacked. All guns were manned and engaged but the Luftwaffe were able to drop 5 bombs on the area, causing some light damage, but no serious issues.

As the sun rose the following morning, the damage caused by the previous night's raid became evident, not only in the town but in the eyes of those who stood and witnessed it. The challenge that faced the fresh arrivals dawned on Gwyn in the morning light as he realised that these horrific raids would continue daily.

The familiar heat of the desert continued to torment Gwyn and his fellow soldiers, with endless streams of sweat saturating their uniforms, causing the moist fabric to hang heavily from their drained, dehydrated bodies. The endless cycle of day-to-day tasks such as cleaning and maintaining equipment would constantly be interrupted by the wail of sirens that warned of another impending attack.

Wave after wave of enemy aircraft crossed the Mediterranean, from one continent to another, bringing with them a swarm of deadly explosives. As the enemy were spotted, sirens would ring out, and each man, highly trained and experienced slipped into a frame of mind that prepared them for battle. An elite ability to switch their Instincts on at a second's notice. They effortlessly aimed and loaded their guns, using the muscle memory and skill they had acquired. Each man seamlessly falling into any role without a single word uttered.

When fire rained down from the deadly enemy raids, the constant state of readiness meant very little needed to change in the town. The few locals that remained would find cover, and the busy streets would empty as each man rushed to their battle stations. But the atmosphere that clung to the air as Gwyn arrived at the town, remained a constant.

As the clusters of Anti-Aircraft shells streamed into the air, the echo of deadly explosions deafened the troops that fired them. The sky became dominated by the glow of each explosion, which Gwyn thought must have been a harrowing sight for the pilots of the incoming bombers.

The enemy planes that made it through the storm

of anti-aircraft fire, targeted the harbour and every shot fired from either side would send smoke and sand into the air. The cloud of dust would envelop the town in a protective cover of a desert mist. Each raid left behind both, a cloud of smoke and sand that took an age to subside, and a team of emboldened gunners.

The raids that haunted Gwyn were relentless, but they varied in strength and purpose. The occasional lone aircraft would fly overhead at high altitudes for reconnaissance and that would account for the night's action. But other nights would bring huge amounts of bombers with the sole purpose of destruction.

Some days remained etched in Gwyn's mind due to the ferocity of the raids. One of these occasions was the 24th of May, when an early reconnaissance flight appeared over the Mediterranean at 1350 hrs. and again at 1746 hrs. These small numbers of aircraft failed to come within range of the AA guns and left without a single shot being fired. This, however, was only a glimpse at what was to follow.

At 2124 hrs. 25 enemy aircrafts appeared on the horizon with deadly intent. They split into their usual unpredictable patterns and dropped down to a low altitude ready to attack. The men of the 175th bty manned their guns with the steely resolve they had adopted. Their determination to defend the vital harbour unwavering.

The intruders dropped their bombs as soon as they could claw themselves into range of any target that may prove troublesome to the German campaign, but the unforgiving defence continued to repel them for more than an hour of intense, back-breaking fighting. Eventually, the Germans relented and withdrew having dropped almost 100 bombs on the area.

The guns still radiated with the heat of battle as the sand and dust began to settle. But the respite for both man and machine was cut short when at 0330 hrs. on the 25th, another 10 aircraft were spotted. Similar to the earlier attack, they dropped low to release their explosives and were met with a solid flurry of defensive fire. The gunners endured the attack and deterred the onslaught.

The early hours of the 25th of May shone light on the devastation caused by the raids. Buildings were reduced to rubble, and craters pierced the ground, but all crucial infrastructure remained intact, which was a testament to the strategic placement of the AA guns and the skill of those who fired them. The previous 12 hours saw over 100 bombs dropped on

Bone, and over 1000 rounds of anti-aircraft shells fired in return.

The Fall of Tunis

Gwyn's continued determination to keep the enemy air forces from putting the harbour of Bone out of action paid off as the Allied ground forces closed in on the pivotal city of Tunis. The Tunisian capital was desperately defended by German and Italian forces, but the relentless determination of the British-American forces continued to dominate the city. They continued to squeeze the struggling Axis forces, pushing them deeper inside the city.

On the 13th of May 1943, the Axis forces eventually relented and surrendered. The Allied forces took over 270,000 prisoners of war from Tunis, each of them a trophy of a magnificent victory. The imprisoned Axis soldiers, now unable to retreat into German or Italian-occupied lands, greatly reduced the capabilities of the enemy for battles to come.

During the campaign in North Africa, almost 400,000 troops were lost or injured. This enormous number is a testament to the fierce battles that raged across the width of a continent and the deadly diseases that thrived. Each yard of Africa that had been prised from evil hands stood as a huge win for the Allies. The continent that sat so close to enemy-occupied Italy provided a foothold in which they could now launch their return to Europe.

As the Allies had succeeded in Africa, the Germans and Italians now realised the importance of preventing a concentration of forces along the northern coast, as an invasion force could spell disaster for their campaign. So, their raids continued, but with greater intensity with the intent of putting the harbour out of use and disrupting any potential mass organisation.

On the 30th of June, the largest raid of Gwyn's time at Bone was seen approaching at 0425 hrs. Over 50 low-flying aircraft viciously bombed Bone, but the 1500 rounds fired in its defence were enough to save the harbour from destruction.

The Aftermath

Only two months after the heroic victory of North Africa, the Allied forces launched a huge amphibious and airborne invasion of the island of Sicily known as 'Operation Husky.'

Gwyn remained at the harbour of Bone as fellow

Allied troops made their final preparations before being thrust back into the crucible of war. Gwyn watched as each battle-worn man stepped upon the ship that would take them to Italy. Each one of their was faces covered in a thick layer of fear and trepidation. He could feel the enormity of the task these men were about to undertake. The atmosphere of readiness had turned to one of urgency. The stern commands of those in charge highlighted the magnitude of the situation.

A mass of troops assembled along the North African coast, ready to cross the Mediterranean and invade the island of Sicily. The collection of troops and ships that had congregated required protection whilst they made final preparations. With Bone so close to Sicily, Gwyn and his unit were key to protecting a portion of these troops.

British intelligence was all too aware of the fierce force that the Germans and Italians would throw at them to halt the invasion. So, with a clever plan, they managed to deceive their enemies.

'Operation Mincemeat' was an ingenious plan of deception where the British intelligence service obtained the body of a homeless man, dressed him up as a Royal Marine officer and planted the corpse in the Mediterranean, off the coast of Spain. The body held fake identification and some correspondence between two British generals suggesting the Allies intended to invade Greece. The corpse found its way into the hands of the Nazis who reacted as the British had hoped. Hitler insisted that Greece must be defended at all costs and began moving valuable resources to the area. By the end of June, the German strength in Greece had doubled, with 18 divisions and the German torpedo boats now based between Greece and the Balkans. By moving a portion of their forces further east, the Axis powers had inadvertently reduced the defensive resources that would stand in the way of the forces that had assembled on the North African coast, thus relieving the pressure on Gwyn to protect them.

The brief respite from the relentless waves of enemy aircraft was welcomed by Gwyn and his unit. They were finally able to take a breath and catch up on some much-needed maintenance. His 3.7-inch Heavy Anti-Aircraft gun had spent days firing endless streams of explosives into the oncoming attacks. It, like him, was exhausted, dirty, and ready for a well-deserved break. But unfortunately for them both, the day-to-day rigours of desert life never stopped. The endless drills and exercises allowed no time for rest.

Although the constant bombardment from above had subsided, the threat of attacks still existed. The air was still filled with the reality of war, with battle now raging only a short Mediterranean journey away. The echoes of war still lingered as Gwyn took a moment to look out over the now-calm water. The feeling of pride and accomplishment for the victory that he'd played his part of was short, as the realisation that although they had conquered the North of Africa, most of continental Europe remained untouched by Allied hands. The Soviet battles in the east were fiercely fought, and progress was slow, but in the west and the south, only the first step was about to be taken.

CHAPTER THIRTEEN

The Italian Job

The British and US forces landed in Sicily in July, and mainland Italy in September 1943. Their hard-fought battle to land and make ground from the south proved to be a gruelling task, with both sides encountering a huge number of casualties. Despite the fierce defence by the Axis forces, the British and US troops made solid gains. Their unrelenting determination to push forward, claiming every inch that lay in front of them proved unstoppable following the invasion.

By the 1st of October, the Allies had captured

Naples, and by the end of the year, they had reached the Gustav line. The Gustav line was a line of defence that the Germans had fallen back to, which ran across the width of Italy. With the south of the country taken, and the Italians who had been liberated, switching sides and declaring war on Germany, concern grew that the south and its vital Allied supply routes could become a target for the German Airforce.

Gwyn and his battery, who continued to catch their breath in Bone, soon received new orders. In December 1943, their commanding officer put them on notice that they were to receive orders to move within the next few hours. The news caused mixed feelings among the men. Despite the relentless heat, sweat and inescapable sand and dust that stuck to everything, Gwyn had grown fond of Northern Africa. Its mix of vibrant life and traditional culture stood in stark contrast to everything he had grown up knowing, but it was the vast contrast that gripped him. He had never had the opportunity to mingle amongst a civilisation as diverse as that of Northern Africa, nor had he any way of digesting such an array of personalities. There was something about the spirit of the people and the fast-paced way of life that filled him with a sense of curiosity. He longed to explore this fascinating place; despite the physical strain it would cause. With those thoughts playing in his mind, there was a small voice at the back of his head teasing the possibility that this summons to an unknown location may turn out the be his ticket home.

Despite the small glimmer of hope that teased him, Gwyn knew that the war was far from over and there were hundreds of miles of land, strongly defended by enemy forces that must be conquered. He maintained a clarity of the overall situation, knowing the only way of seeing his family at peace again, was to defeat the Germans.

The time came for the men who once defended the African coast to sail away from it. They boarded a ship with apprehension and nerves. Their few personal treasures were safely tucked in their pockets and their army-issued belongings stuck tightly to their back. As the ship departed the harbour, Gwyn watched as the golden sands of Bone shrank out of sight and he gently floated on the calm waters of the Mediterranean.

The journey soon brought the sight of a new horizon. A rugged coastline grew in the distance, a land alien to Gwyn. As the men aboard, that lazed upon any surface that lay flat, began to rise and voices grew louder, Gwyn looked out over the incoming land. He noticed the icy tips of distant mountains and the beautiful stone buildings imprinted within the coast. The cooler temperature was a stark reminder that they were no longer in the deserts of Africa.

The Adriatic

After disembarking on Italian soil, and some long, bone-rattling journeys along the war-ravaged land, Gwyn eventually arrived at Manfredonia. Manfredonia is a small, picturesque harbour town on the east coast of Italy. It sits about 80 miles north of Bari and overlooks the Adriatic Sea. On the 2nd of December 1943, German bombers attacked the larger port of Bari, catching its defenders by surprise. The brutal attack lasted over an hour and destroyed at least 27 ships. The attack put the harbour out of action, causing problems in getting personnel and supplies to the front line. With Manfredonia a short distance north, it was selected for the 175th bty HQ. From here, Gwyn would be able to defend the Adriatic coast from any future raids from the Balkans.

Upon arrival, Gwyn noticed the stark contrast between the colourful Mediterranean scenery and the characterless white buildings that sat on the dusty rocks of Africa. The vibrant design of the town, however, was not left undamaged by the raging war. Some buildings had been reduced to rubble; others had been burned to ash. The suffering didn't stop with buildings. Lives had been destroyed, brothers, sisters, mothers, and fathers had been killed or forced to fight a war alongside Nazi Germany, with whom they shared no common interests or ideologies.

The civilians that remained in Manfredonia were painfully suffering. They had lost their homes, businesses, and families. They lived in the streets and ate scraps like stray animals. Each person deciding if the small fist full of bread they had been tossed by a British soldier should be selfishly eaten now to ensure their own survival or shared carefully amongst others. Their businesses had either been destroyed or taken over by the Allied soldiers to utilise for their own needs.

Some of the American troops that were posted in the area, showed no sympathy towards the innocent lives that had been ruined. Their view of the political situation that gripped Italy was that these 'innocent' civilians had supported a fascist dictator in Benito Mussolini, and it was he who sided with the Germans and allowed the war to escalate. They believed that each civilian had a choice but had simply made the wrong one and now had to accept the consequences.

These American troops were Allies and brothers of war to Gwyn. They had to fight shoulder-to-shoulder to prevail. They had to trust and believe in each other. But it was small groups of men, like these, that left a bad taste for the Americans in his mouth. The arrogance and lack of empathy and compassion for those whose lives they had helped destroy, planted the seed of animosity between them. Gwyn's understanding of the turmoil that swept over Italy was more sympathetic. He knew that these innocent civilians never chose this life of starvation and pain. They simply want to live comfortably and be happy. His open-minded attitude would clash with American troops as he tried to explain that the soldiers and civilians on both sides of the war were victims of the greedy individuals who ruled over them. Even the most loyal and devoted German soldier would rather be at home with his family, but they, like Gwyn, were following orders. To say the Italian civilians were to blame for their own misfortune was to say those lost during the German bombing raids over Britain were to blame for choosing to be British. The only difference was that the war came to the Italian's doorstep.

Those animated exchanges, along with the calls of 'Limeys' from the Americans, painted a picture that Gwyn could never erase. He disliked the American he served with, and once that thought had embedded into his mind, there was no changing it. He once, controversially, admitted that he had more respect for the German soldiers that endlessly attempted to take his life, than those American soldiers that he called 'Brothers.' The German soldiers, similar to the British, were simply following orders. They never attempted to decipher what was right from wrong, as their duty was to their own country and deciding what was morally correct was for those that held the positions to do so. The Germans understood that, and possibly respected it too. The American troops that Gwyn served with seemed to struggle to comprehend that good and evil were subjective, depending on which side of the battlefield you stood.

The first few days on Italian soil were a chaotic medley of reorganisation and construction. Although there was a small number of military facilities in the town, they were massively insufficient and underdeveloped for the incoming defensive troops. The gun sites needed for the colossal Anti-Aircraft guns needed work too. The sites needed flattening, the guns needed construction, and their bunkers needed preparing. This work was rapidly done, with Gwyn and his team relentlessly working to get operational.

The cold winter months that Gwyn endured were spent defending the coast from the unforgiving enemy air forces and the significance of the harbour was not lost on him. He understood that the Allies could not afford to endure another horrific attack like the one on Bari, as the front-line troops desperately needed the equipment and reinforcements that the coast welcomed. As well as the harbour, Manfredonia sat twenty miles east of Foggia. Foggia was the home of the 'Foggia Airfield Complex' which was a vast group of Airfields that the US Airforce and the RAF utilised for their heavy bombing campaigns in Europe. From Foggia, they could reach Germany, France, Austria, and the Balkans, which were inaccessible from England. Amongst this complex was also the Adriatic command centre. So, having an experienced Anti-Aircraft regiment on the coast nearby was a vital resource for the Allies.

The Raids

During the early winter months of 1944, raids over the Adriatic coast came from the Balkans. With the gun position overlooking the sea, the hum of enemy aircraft echoed through the air and the once-still water began to ripple. As the waves of aircraft approached, Gwyn and his fellow soldiers would be manning their weapons. They would be aimed and loaded, waiting for the enemy to fly into range before unleashing their shells.

As the spring skies cleared, giving perfect conditions for air raids, the intensity increased. The frequency and ferocity of the raids concerned the Allies. They knew that the Luftwaffe were exhausted. They knew the Nazi's production of aircraft had slowed and those that they did have were spread far too thinly across Europe. So, the sudden increase in aircraft numbers suggested a concentration of enemy forces in the Balkans and that made the potential for an invasion, on the east coast of Italy, likely.

In April of 1944, the British and US air forces began a heavy bombing campaign of the Balkans. They relentlessly attacked supply lines, transport networks and industrial infrastructure to disrupt any potential for a gathering invasion force. This, in turn, reduced the incoming enemy raids, allowing Gwyn some respite. These moments of downtime were enjoyed in the picturesque towns and the facilities provided by the vast Airforce complex nearby.

The animosity and tension between the British and the Americans within the camp created an environment that forced the small groups of friends and colleagues closer, strengthening their bonds further. Gwyn and his fellow gunners bonded over their common discomfort around the US troops, but despite that, they continued to work side by side to achieve their goals.

CHAPTER FOURTEEN

Back in Training

With the new aerial offensive pinning back any significant raids, the needs of the Allied forces in Italy had evolved, and by the summer of 1944, there were an excess of defensive units on the Adriatic coast. In contrast to the Anti-Aircraft units, the frontline ground forces were suffering a major shortage of manpower. The huge losses that the infantry units had taken began to take their toll and progress began to slow. The front line desperately needed reinforcements and the men of the Anti-Aircraft units were the obvious choice.

On the 3rd of July 1944, Gwyn received orders that

would again change the path of his military career, as well as his personal life. The monumental change that loomed over him filled him with fear. Each man who received the order felt the same. Some put on a brave face and refused to admit their concerns, but as Gwyn looked into their eyes, he could sense the same trepidation that he battled with.

The commanding officer explained their unit would soon be relieved by the incoming African Anti-Aircraft units that were newly trained and inexperienced. The 85th HAA regiment, that Gwyn had been an integral part of since the beginning of 1940, would be disbanded in the winter and he would be amongst the first wave of gunners to be transferred out immediately.

Gwyn had little time to pack his things and say his goodbyes to those that he would leave behind. Over the last 4 years, the men he had spent every minute of the day alongside had become brothers. They shared laughs, successes, losses, and everything in between. The bond that had been forged in the turmoil of war carried them through the most difficult times of their lives. Moments of fear and weakness shared during the dark times helped them feel reassured that they were never alone.

Gwyn's days in the Royal Artillery came to an end as he arrived in Cervinara, east of Naples, where a sprawling camp of tents, stone structures and rugged terrain was home to thousands of troops. Gwyn was transferred to the Hampshire Regiment that were fighting furiously on the front line towards the north of Italy. They had taken huge losses in their campaign and urgently needed reinforcements for their push on the Gothic line. The camp that Gwyn was now a part of was an IRTD (Infantry retraining depot).

Gwyn was a hugely experienced soldier with a vast knowledge of weaponry and tactical warfare, he had faced brutal combat in the most difficult situations anyone could have faced. He had stared deep into the abyss and still continued to fight onwards. Despite the wealth of experience he had, this training camp was no walk in the park.

The first couple of days were dedicated to the adjustment of the newly integrated troops. They would have to adapt to new uniforms, weapons, regulations and learn the standards required of infantrymen. Each man had recently been transferred from various units from across the globe, their face mirroring the pain and losses they had endured but being thrust into a new world allowed them no time to recover either physically or mentally.

Hardly 48 hours had passed before orders were being barked and drills were being called. Gwyn had barely had the opportunity to lace up his newly issued boots when he was ordered to the parade ground for the rigorous regime of training.

Once adequate levels of physical fitness had been established, the true tactics and intricacies of frontline ground warfare were explored. Gwyn was drilled relentlessly with the manoeuvres and signals he would need to master in order to survive the brutal conflict that stood in his way. He worked around the clock at his marksmanship, ensuring his rifle was the deadly tool it needed to be.

Naples

With training dominating Gwyn's days, he was spared little respite, but during periods of poor weather or the short spells of rest between drills, Gwyn and his new colleagues would be required to assist in Naples.

The Allies captured Naples in October 1943 but

were initially disappointed upon arriving. They believed Naples to be a momentous milestone. Its infrastructure and facilities promised to be a vital foothold in the battle into the north of Italy. However, as they entered the city, very little was left standing. It had been virtually destroyed, with buildings and bridges reduced to rubble. The Allies had shelled the city heavily during the campaign to force the Germans to withdraw, causing major damage, but what they didn't expect was the destruction that the German forces had added before withdrawing. They removed or destroyed all communication, water, power, and transport facilities. They burned hotels, destroyed train stations and sunk all ships that sat in the harbour. The German rampage accounted for most of the damage that swept across the city.

Almost a year had passed since the Germans had withdrawn, and the Allies had worked tirelessly to restore the city's essential requirements. Although it was almost fully functional by the time Gwyn's service there was needed, there was still work to do. Rubble still lined the streets within parts of the city and buildings still required repairing. Looking over the harbour that once sat in ruins, Gwyn contemplated the state of such a historical place. He would wonder if Naples had endured the last of the conflict that would be asked of it. He was hopeful that it had, but uncertainty lingered in his mind.

Friends

The few moments of peace Gwyn found overlooking the gentle swell within the Gulf of Naples were spent alongside men that he had forged friendships with during the rigours of training. They would speak of the horrors they had faced in various theatres of war and the dread they felt for battles that loomed in the not-so-distant future. These bonds held the potential both to save and destroy Gwyn's morale. A friendship that endured the suffering of war was one that a man would sacrifice his life for, but on the other hand, each close bond formed was another heartbreaking loss that he may have to accept. Friends like these were vital for survival during dark times, and none more vital to Gwyn than the friendships he forged with Jim and Bill.

Jim, a young man around the same age as Gwyn, had a slight physique that stood a couple of inches shorter. His thick, jet-black hair, always immaculate, framed a characterful face. Even during the darkest of times when there was nothing to smile about, he maintained a glimmer in his eye that radiated joy. His smile would brighten a room, and his personality matched. His warm, comforting nature and booming Lancashire accent stood as a reassuring presence and his company always made Gwyn feel at ease in any situation.

Bill completed the trio with his dry, sarcastic sense of humour. He would make light of any situation regardless of how dire it had become. The timing of his jokes could often be considered inappropriate by those who didn't know him, but Gwyn and Jim loved his light, bubbly personality. They knew he meant no offence by anything he said, he was far too charismatic and charming to offend, and his humour was the coping mechanism he had developed for uncomfortable situations. He was the taller of the three and his light hair would blow thinly in the breeze.

The three men became inseparable from their time in Naples onwards. They would chat, laugh, and cry together. They shared their fears, hopes for the future, and spoke about their families. They became brothers. Not in the same sense that Gwyn and the Americans were brothers of war, but nearer to that of biological brothers. They developed a relationship closer to the one shared between Gwyn, Glyn, Vincent and Keith, which Gwyn cherished and missed so dearly. They would slowly earn a reputation as the jokers. They would laugh and pull lighthearted practical jokes around the barracks, creating mischief and bringing moments of joy when it was needed.

A New Challenge

13 weeks of hard work and dedication to his new skills meant that Gwyn was now ready for the terror that lurked in the north. The new bonds he had to form with fellow infantrymen would soon be rigorously tested by the grim reality of battle.

With training completed, and the front line desperate for support, orders for Gwyn's next mission became clear. He was posted to the 2/4th battalion of the Hampshire Regiment on the 6th of October 1944 and ordered to head north towards the Gothic line and support the Allied assault.

Gwyn travelled over 300 miles into northern Italy and back to the Adriatic coast. He joined the men of the 2/4th who were billeted south of the River Merecchia near Rimini. Arriving as part of a wave of reinforcements sent to replace the men killed or captured during the latest Allied onslaught, Gwyn sensed the sombre atmosphere that stained the faces and uniforms of his new colleagues. Their troubled minds seeping into their every word and expression. Stepping into these new barracks with their pristine uniform and rested posture was an uncomfortable experience for the newcomers, a feeling of guilt and sorrow consumed them. Gwyn pondered what the men must be feeling, having a man that you have never met before, sleeping in a bed that once belonged to a dear friend who had been brutally killed. The feeling that a close friend and brother could be heartlessly replaced by 50 other men at the click of an officer's finger, must play on their minds. They must have felt disposable. Despite their silent reflection, these psychologically exhausted men understood their situation. They would soon be facing their next brutal battle, and they knew that they needed the fresh-faced reinforcements to survive.

Seven miles south of Rimini is Riccione, and between the two is the Frederico Fellini airport. Although it is now a sizeable international airport, at the time it was little more than a military airdrome. It held no importance in the terms of aerial warfare, but following the battle of Rimini in the September of 1944, the month prior to Gwyn's arrival, it was taken by the Allies and used as a prisoner-of-war camp. The camp held up to 80,000

German troops at any one time, but due to the severe manpower shortage at the front line, just to the north, it was poorly guarded, and escapes were common.

The battle of Rimini saw the Allies forcing the Germans to withdraw with a devastating series of attacks. The city was hit by 373 air raids and almost 1.5 million rounds were fired by the Allied ground forces. Upon entry to the city, British officers estimated that less than 2 per cent of buildings remained standing.

Gwyn bore witness to the devastation. The city lay in ruins with some buildings still smouldering in the cooling autumn air. The rebuilding had begun, but with less urgency than he had expected. The main priority was the front line, and all resources were directed towards it. Rimini was filled with temporary structures and open-air facilities, but despite the military's best efforts, it was unable to entertain the concentration of troops stationed in and around the city. Riccione, which stood on the southern side of the POW camp, was also utilised during times of rest and recreational breaks. As most soldiers of the battalion were in recovery following the recent battles, there were numerous shows and pictures shown in both Rimini and

Riccione, which allowed Gwyn to integrate with his new comrades.

These moments of recuperation were welcomed by Gwyn and the other men as the incoming tide of war rumbled in the distance. In moments that Gwyn felt himself beginning to relax, a stark reminder of the fight would rear its ugly head. With the battle for territory ongoing only 30 miles to the northwest, the distant rumbles of explosives and the orange glow of fire lit the horizon. Troops that had been relieved from the front line would withdraw with their blood-stained uniforms and pictures of horror painted on their dirty faces. In these moments, Gwyn would remember why he was there and contemplated what the near future had in store for him.

CHAPTER FIFTEEN

The Advance on Forli

Soon after Gwyn's arrival near the front line, torrential and relentless rain struck hard. Being from Wales, Gwyn was no stranger to the wet weather and the issues that arose with it, but this was like nothing he had ever experienced and the partially built structures were washed away by streams of rainwater.

The north of Italy is crossed by hundreds of streams and rivers of different strengths and sizes, each one of which provided the Germans with a line of defence. Each loss they suffered saw them retreat beyond the next river and set up their defences. Those same rivers became milestones for the Allies. Securing a crossing over these rivers represented a small but important victory.

Gwyn and his new 2/4th Btn were soon to be called into battle. They were given orders to move forward on the 26th of October 1944 toward the town of Forli which was occupied by the Germans. This would be Gwyn's first taste of combat as an infantry soldier alongside men he had not served with before. He didn't know their strengths or weaknesses but had to trust that they were as well motivated and as trustworthy as he was. The advance became fixed in his mind. Each action of preparation was dominated by the focus he possessed for his mission. However, somewhat disappointingly, the order for the attack on Forli was postponed as word from the front had filtered back that the river Ronco, which guarded Forli, was flowing far too quickly and its levels had risen far too high for the infantry to cross. Although this news gave Gwyn more time to mentally prepare himself, the anxiety of what was to come festered within him until the 30th of October when he received the news that he had been nervously waiting for. They were to move on the 1st of November.

Indeed, the 1st came and finally, as expected, they moved forward. They moved quickly to the city of Cesena around 15 miles short of Forli. Here, they joined a concentration of troops preparing to move forward to relieve the exhausted men that were battling on the front. Later in the day, news filtered its way through the channels of command to Gwyn's ears. The 10-infantry brigade had managed to cross the river Ronco and were now at the outskirts of Forli. The stories that were coming back from the river were ones of terror. The resistance that the Germans were showing was a sign that this would be a bloody episode of warfare.

The 2/4th remained in Cesena while the 10-infantry brigade continued to knock on the door of Forli. The inability of the artillery or tanks to cross the river due to its levels made for difficult progress and for that reason, the 2/4th waited for the water levels of the river to drop. Mercifully, on the 8th of November, the rain eased, and the river levels allowed a fully committed advance to the city.

At 0350 Hrs. Gwyn moved to Selbagnone just to the southeast of the river Ronco that guarded Forli, where they encountered heavy, long-range shelling. They replied with their own barrage of shell fire, each explosion was deafening. The cold wet ground, which had been chewed up by the heavy impact it had received, was sprayed into the air, covering the sheltering men in layers of thick mud. The weight of their dirty, damp clothes and boots made it difficult to move. With their mobility reduced, responding to each barrage became increasingly difficult but they continued to battle on. The overpowering stench of burning metal filled Gwyn's nostrils, it was not a smell he was unfamiliar with, but mixed with the cold, moist air and the layers of loose soil now lying over his face, it was a stark realisation of the new theatre of war he had now entered.

The exchange continued for hours. With neither side blinking, the continuous back and forth remained as intense as the very first shell fired. The first major punch landed during the early stages of Gwyn's new campaign was a direct hit landed on the 2/4th at 1030 hrs. on the 8th of November. The horrific moment saw over 50 people perish including a captain, lieutenant, 2 other ranking officers and a chaplain. Gwyn was newly acquainted with these men, but the loss he felt for his fellow soldiers was immense. He understood the feeling of losing someone he was close to, but the death of a commanding officer felt personal.

The men, inspired and enraged by the direct hit continued to battle on.

The shelling had eased by 1055 hrs. allowing a moment of solitude for the 2/4th. Utilising this pause in hostilities, one of the remaining officers left for the brigade HQ to request replacements for the specialised officials, equipment, and stores that the exchange had lost. These replacements were issued immediately in order to maintain the forward momentum they had built. The newly appointed official that took control of the 2/4th at 1800 hrs. insisted they would continue to move forward and join the assault across the river despite the blow they had received.

By midnight, reports suggested that there were signs that the enemy were withdrawing from the city of Forli. Sensing an opportunity to achieve their goals of capturing the city, the new officials ordered the move forward immediately and by 0710 Hrs. the first Allied pioneer units entered the city to clear mines with the infantry following closely behind at 0720 hrs. Another company, entering the town further north, reported sniper fire and signalled to the 2/4th to be vigilant. Stepping through the cobblestone streets of a city lined with the litter of battle was airy, and the enemy threat of a deadly marksman tracing his movement frightened Gwyn. Each step he took risked the possibility of death. Each corner he turned may offer a glimmer of a target through the snipers' sites. The thick gloomy mist that filled the air, should have reassured Gwyn that the conditions didn't favour a sniper. But the poor visibility only filled him with further dread.

Few enemy troops were encountered in Forli, but those that were sighted posed no threat. The white rags that blew innocently on their raised rifles indicated they had no fight left in them. It signalled the end of their war as they were apprehended by the Allies and sent back to the poorly guarded POW camp near Rimini. Gwyn watched as these men stumbled towards him, their pale skin coloured only by blood and dirt. Their torn uniform dragged behind them as they painfully limped forward. He considered how desperate and defeated they must have felt to give up everything they had fought for and surrender themselves to the hands of their enemy. He thought about what would need to happen in the coming days, weeks, months or even years for him to surrender himself to the hands of the men so desperate to kill him. He could think of no scenario that he would not fight on until the bitter end, but that same thought made him question if he or the terrified German prisoners had the most sound understanding of the situation.

The next 12 hours in the city saw a tirade of increasingly deadly shellfire from the west. The Germans had retreated beyond their next defensive river and had set up their artillery positions at the river Montone. Gwyn sheltered within a stable-looking building for the night and listened intently to each round of shellfire that shattered the streets around him. The hours of darkness lit up by the yellow flash of explosions.

On to The Next Objective

In the early hours of the morning on the 11th of November, 2 patrols moved forward from Forli towards the river Montone. Their task was to defend the river and prevent the Germans from regrouping, recrossing, and retaking Forli. Gwyn, mentally preparing to follow these 2 patrols into battle, had worked up the courage to accept his next mission with readiness, assuming his fate had already been sealed. His premeditated ideas of the next battle were interrupted as word came through that the 2/4th would be relieved the following day. The 2/4th blew a collective breath of relief as the fierce German shelling overnight suggested they were prepared for another bloody battle. The prospect of relief meant some dry clothes, a meal, some sleep and perhaps another wave of reinforcements to replenish those who never made it to Forli.

Gwyn and the 2/4th withdrew to southeast Forli in the afternoon of the 12th where they were out of range of the German artillery fire. Here, they regrouped and reorganised both kit and leadership, with permanent replacements being appointed to lead the unit. On the 14th they were on the move again under orders to secure positions at Villafranca under heavy mortaring. They achieved their goal and prepared for their next mission of establishing a bridgehead over the river Montone, but heavy rain once again put a stop to the plan, and they were relieved back to Forli. They remained at Forli for another 9 days before being called forward again. This time, the relentless Allied assault had pushed the Germans further from the safety of the river Montone and were set up beyond the river Cosina further west.

At 0900 hrs. on the 21st, Gwyn was ordered to march west towards the frontline for the final time. His experiences of frontline duty were eye-opening and the sights and sounds he had witnessed were ones of horror that would never be forgotten, but the relentless pursuit of progress by the military gave him no opportunity for self-pity. Emotions of a negative nature would get him killed on the battlefield and he knew it. Gwyn needed the steely resilience and resolve that he relied on so heavily during his childhood and the early days at war. The personality traits of strength and endurance he had developed would continue to be tested despite his mind having defeated each task it had faced, and this challenge would be no different.

River Cosina

The 2/4th arrived at a concentrated area just east of the river Cosina at 1100 hrs. on the 22nd of November and had set up their HQ by 1400 hrs. Once established, the men were briefed on their mission details. They would advance to the front line and secure two houses that were believed to be occupied by enemy units. As Gwyn and his 2/4th stood at the Allied defensive line preparing to bravely move beyond it, a sudden downpour of shells and mortars rained down upon them. The makeshift defence that had been swiftly constructed along the line helped protect Gwyn and the small group of men that congregated around him, but others, believing they were beyond the range of the Germans, roamed freely in the open space that had been created by previous battles, and painfully perished in the blasts. The already stretched 2/4th Btn had lost the lives of even more valued soldiers, plus the casualties that would be evacuated to the safety of a nearby military hospital. The losses only motivated Gwyn and the men to reach their goal. The desire that burned inside them, fuelled by pain and anger, would be the motivation that marched them over the hostile terrain towards the enemy.

As the now fired-up men moved beyond the false safety of their own defensive line, they faced a landscape of dark brown craters carved into the treacherous slopes. The rugged terrain was a testament to the barrage of explosives the land had faced, and each shell had ingrained itself into the history of the land.

They moved forward towards their target under the shadows of shellfire. With every clumsy dart towards the next shape that roughly resembled something close to shelter, they dodged the moving earth that exploded in front of them. Shells fell all around them, throwing debris into the air. With the recent tragedy fresh in his mind, Gwyn continued the gradual progress across the battlefield.

With the two houses coming into view in the distance. The sound of rifle fire rang through the air. Bullets whistled past Gwyn's head, and the warm air following them blew on his cheek as he raised from safety to take a shot and dash for the next foothold on the battlefield. The 2/4th continued moving forward, clambering over their fallen friends who lay still in the dirt, desperately using their lifeless bodies for cover. The continued advance proved unstoppable as by 1900 hrs. their objective had been completed and the houses had been secured. As a patrol continued forward beyond the houses to ensure the Germans were withdrawing beyond shelling range, Gwyn helped round up the huge number of prisoners of war that had surrendered during the battle. During this exchange, more than 120 German POWs had been taken, and they continued to arrive in droves with their rifles held high above their heads.

The Second Phase

The darkness came with a wave of silence as the withdrawing enemy scurried to safety. Apart from his short stint on watch, Gwyn's night was restful. It was rest that he and his fellow soldiers desperately needed to provide the strength needed to achieve their next goal.

As daylight broke over the bullet-riddled houses that the men had hunkered down in, the landscape spoke of the true horror that had come before, but there was no time to dwell on the previous day's conflict, as in the early hours of the 23rd the troops were briefed on their next objective. Later in the day, they were to move forward once more to capture another two houses and finally secure a bridgehead over the river Cosina.

The morning was spent with the busy clatter of preparation filling the air. Gwyn packed the essentials, checking and rechecking he had everything he would need for each scenario he imagined he could face. His boots and uniform had begun to dry through the night but still clung heavily to his body. He checked his rifle for any potential issues he could face at the pivotal moment that he needed it most, cleaning it and rechecking it over and over. He methodically checked his ammunition and organised it upon his person in a way that muscle memory could reach and reload during the heat of battle.

At 1400 hrs. the order was made for the 2/4th to advance. The already destroyed terrain was damaged further by the retreating German troops. The saturated ground proved difficult to move through, but Gwyn waded through the ice-cold water that had pooled within the craters that lined the battlefield. The collision between the fierce shells and the moist earth shook the ground around him. The continued advance by the Allies allowed little time for the enemy to regroup and assemble their artillery, but they did manage to quickly put together a defence that was able to fire a few rounds, which caused little concern for the 2/4th.

A weakened opposition engaged from the target houses. Their numbers, significantly less than that of the previous encounter, underlined the success of the advance. They defended mostly with machine gun fire, with desperate individual soldiers firing their rifles over their heads whilst sheltering out of sight. Their efforts waned as the gap closed. The picture painted was one of defeat for the Germans and they knew it. The majority of troops fled over the river that the Allies had come to secure, disappearing out of sight over the Cosina. Few stood and fought until the end but those that did were quickly killed or captured. By 1620 hrs. both houses and the bridgehead had been captured. The Germans had taken huge losses and those that had survived had desperately withdrawn. Despite heavy Allied losses, the operation was painted as a resounding success. Large numbers of POWs were taken and more continued to appear from over the bridge both on foot and on stretchers.

Intelligence filtering back suggests the Germans had retreated beyond the river Lamone at the east of the city of Faenza. The withdrawal created an extended gap between the opponents, which put both armies out of range of the other's deadly artillery. Knowing this, the men were able to take some time to regroup and collect their thoughts. The rumbles of war echoed in the distance, but those murmurs were little more than white noise to those who had endured 5 years of war. Amongst those was Gwyn, who watched as the sun set over the river. Grateful that he had escaped death once more.

Mission Accomplished

Knowing the 2/4th had taken huge losses, Gwyn knew that reinforcements must be pushed forward before they would be able to advance further. They could not maintain the intensity of their attacks with the numbers they held. His intuition proved correct, as at 1000 hrs. on the 25th of November, news came that a fresh group of men would be joining them. However, these would not be reinforcements, but relief. The 2/4th were to fall back to Forli as soon as their replacements had arrived.

By 1330 hrs. they were on the move, retracing the terrain that remained a stark reminder of the hell they had endured. They arrived back at Forlì by 1530 hrs. and were told they had just completed their last objective in Italy. The vague information that came as a surprise to Gwyn, stood as a reminder of the fluidity of warfare. The unknown destination to which they would be sent next remained a mystery, but they were told to prepare to move south. South was away from the front line and each man in the 2/4th responded positively to the news.

At 0800 hrs. the following morning of the 26th seen Gwyn board a Troop carrier vehicle (TCV), that was most commonly a Bedford QL, which would carry him and his close comrades back in the direction from which they came. They passed back through Cesena and Rimini before heading south down the Adriatic coast to a staging area set up at Port Civitanova where they stayed for the night.

Again, at 0800 hrs. on the 27th, they boarded another TCV and moved through Pedcara, Ortona and San Vito Chietino before turning inland and arriving at Lanciano at 1300 hrs. Once they arrived, they were given new uniforms and equipment and told to prepare to move at the start of December. Despite the location to which they would move remaining classified, the men would share whispers from their bunks. The fresh uniform they had been issued suggested warmer weather, and with the current political situation, the assumption was the Middle East.

As 1944 was coming to an end, the uncertainty in Gwyn's life remained a constant. The 2nd of December came, and orders were given for the men to move. They were to leave by rail at 1715 hrs. and continue south down the Adriatic coast. The trip was long but pleasant. At this point in the war, Gwyn and the men would have taken the opportunity to sit somewhere comfortably, whilst remaining dry, warm and at peace, with both hands.

Arriving at Taranto, in the southeast of Italy, at 1730 hrs. on the 3rd of December, the men were then marched 3 and a half miles to the nearest staging area where they were to set up their camp and await orders. However, officials soon confirmed that a planned move to the Middle East had been postponed and passes were granted for men to visit Taranto each day after 1400 hrs. These passes came with the opportunity for relaxation and exploration. They came with freedom and each man, including Gwyn, Jim, and Bill, were determined not to waste them. Days spent enjoying the historic streets and harbour were interrupted only for brief periods as the 8-mile marches and training drills consumed each morning.

A week spent in relative luxury came to an end on the 10th of December when Gwyn was ordered to prepare to move on the 12th when they would be flown to Greece.

CHAPTER SIXTEEN

Greece

The German occupation of Greece from April 1941 to October 1944 was brutal for both the Greek people and the German soldiers that occupied the country. During the occupation, various resistance parties were created, including the communist-backed EAM, armed with their military branch called the ELAS, who fought relentlessly to end the German occupation. These rebel groups were supplied with weapons and ammunition by the British, who also trained the resistance fighters.

In 1944, with the Axis forces being finely stretched

throughout Europe, Hitler ordered his officials to withdraw from Greece. A proud achievement for the rebel groups, but little time was spent celebrating. With all opposition now defeated, the resistance groups grew into political parties and began to wrestle for control.

As the Germans withdrew, the EAM declared their own government from the Greek mountains, disowning the Greek king and his government, who were in exile. In an attempt to avoid a civil war, the British brought both the communist and royalist groups together to form a coalition government.

Predictably, the coalition fell apart within weeks as the communist EAM party refused to disband their guerrilla forces. A bitter civil war broke out on the 3rd of December with the EAM's guerrilla forces, the ELAS, over-running the city of Athens.

A British Arrival

At 0900 hrs. on the 12th of December 1944, the wheels of a B-24 Liberator pulled up from the runway at Grottaglie airport with Gwyn on board. The B-24 Liberator was a large bomber that had been converted during the later stages of the war into a troop carrier. The size made it a comfortable aircraft for troops to travel on. Gwyn's flight was described as 'smooth' and 'very pleasant.'

The Liberator drifted through the air with ease while Gwyn sat with his back resting on the cold steel shell of the aircraft. The vibrations ran up his spine and the rhythmic hum of the engines drowned out the casual chatter from the men that remained awake. Others sat with their heads slumped forward breathing heavily as they dozed innocently.

The windowless shell of the aircraft was dim, lit only by the beams of light that snuck through the mesh panels that were mounted behind the pilots. The steel benches that had been mounted along the cargo deck would vibrate on the solid supports, creating a metallic knocking that echoed faintly.

The Liberator landed at Kalamaki airfield, known today as Ellinikon international Airport, near Athens at 1230 hrs. The cargo doors of the aircraft lowered, and the bright light beamed in. As the men disembarked in orderly lines, they were greeted by officials of the 4-infantry division. The 2/4th, keen to support their British counterparts, were gathered and briefed. They were told of the current situation within Athens, which filled the new arrivals with concern.

The 4-infantry division held parts of the city, but the ELAS army still held the majority of areas. Although the ELAS rebels only accounted for approximately 10 per cent of the population of Greece, the remainder were being terrorised into cooperation with the threat of arms. In the areas where the ELAS were absent in Athens, the civilians were very friendly and only too happy to help the British.

The officials continued with some stern warnings. They emphasised that the ELAS forces were unlike any army that the 2/4th had faced so far. They were not regular soldiers, and this was not a regular battlefield. They did not wear uniforms, they dressed as any other civilian would, and blended in seamlessly. Their attacks would mostly consist of sniping and machine gun fire before disappearing amongst the population. They had roadblocks lining most of the streets creating perfect environments for an ambush.

The ELAS were very well armed and were dangerously capable in the operation of their weapons. This was not surprising as they had been armed and trained by the British, plus they inherited the large volumes of weapons and ammunition that the Germans had left behind following their withdrawal.

Gwyn listened intently, knowing that any crumb of information he could absorb from these experienced officers may, one day, save his life. He fixed his gaze solidly on one of the men that spoke with intensity. The official finished his briefing by reiterating the nature of this war. The ELAS were dangerous. This was guerrilla warfare, where the rules and laws of war did not apply. They shot at ambulances, they sniped troops that attended to the wounded in the street and almost every vehicle they drove was marked with the Red Cross flag, creating a moral dilemma when deciphering help from hostile.

First Days in Athens

As orders were made for the freshly transferred 2/4th to remain at the airdrome where they had landed, Gwyn and his comrades replayed the briefing in their heads. He had grown accustomed to the flexibility and fluidity of war, as he had faced different challenges on different fronts and had successfully adapted each time. However, he knew the warfare he was about to be drawn into was unlike anything else he had faced. There was no training manual or shortcuts for the type of combat that he was to expect. There were no rules and regulations. Gwyn knew with confidence that he and the 2/4th were far better trained and drilled than the rebels and knew if they were to stand toe to toe with the ELAS, they would dominate any theatre of war. However, the rebel troops knew and understood that too, and because of that, they hid in the shadows. It was because of that they relied on guerrilla warfare and hit-and-run tactics. The fact that the British were superior on all fronts was what made the ELAS dangerous.

Upon arrival in Greece, Gwyn was ordered to remain at the airfield at which he had just arrived where the 2/4th would take over the defence of the complex as there were reports that an attack from the north was being planned. First, they constructed their makeshift camp within the perimeter of the airfield. The camp consisted of some basic tents that would only just be sufficient for the men to sleep in. Once the rudimental camp was set up, they could continue with the mission in hand.

As an accomplished and experienced battalion, the 2/4th were efficient and effective in their mission, quickly establishing patrol routes around the perimeter in order to deter any potential attacks.

They then established a defence system of alarms that would be triggered by any breach of the perimeter and communications lines were set up throughout the airfield to enable a comprehensive system of relaying information from lookouts and guard posts to a central command Centre.

Almost as soon as these tasks were complete, news came in that the 2/4th were to be relieved, as their elite skills would be required for another, more dangerous, objective. With the unit due to relieve the 2/4th scheduled to arrive on the 15th of December, plans were made and briefings were given on their target, however, delays in the arrival of the incoming unit meant the mission was delayed for 24 hours and now would be executed on the 16th, but the issues continued as the relief didn't arrive until late afternoon, so the mission was again pushed on to the 17th.

Fighting the Rebels

After the eventual arrival of their relieving counterparts, Gwyn and the 2/4th moved directly to their post at Faliron near the centre of Athens in preparations for the next morning's mission, so, when the first hint of sunlight began to appear over the historic city of Athens, Gwyn and his team would be ready to act.

The final mission briefing that was given the night before, underlined the severity of the task in hand. The commanding officers emphasised the need to be swift and silent in their preparations. These words echoed in Gwyn's ears as his thoughts wrestled between rest and readiness. His dozing head listened intently for the call to prepare. His closed eyes flickered in anticipation of the light breaking and the shadows lifting. His restless night eventually came to an end just before 0500 hrs. when the men naturally rose with a nervous energy that reverberated through the camp.

They swiftly and stealthily moved to positions only feet from the Brewery they were targeting. They waited for Z hour, planned for 0700 hrs. Intelligence suggested that this Brewery in the heart of Athens was a stronghold of the ELAS forces, and there was a possibility that it was also being used as a rebel arsenal. The building had been covertly watched and studied with extreme caution in preparation for the mission and the stakes were high.

At 0655 hrs. two tanks moved into position before blasting a hole through the side of the building. As the dust and debris flew through the air, the pioneer unit rushed in to set pile charges on the main door, which flung open in the explosion. Within seconds of the first action, snipers opened fire from nests overlooking the street that Gwyn and his comrades were racing through. They dodged the deadly shots and reached the brewery with perfect timing and piled in through the gaping void. The men swiftly moved through the building and within minutes every member of the ELAS forces inside were either killed or captured.

The mission was a resounding success, a testament to the methodical planning and rigorous preparation. Men on the ground worked as efficiently as expected, with zero errors. The result of capturing the brewery gave the Allies 30 prisoners to interrogate and a mixed assortment of weapons including thirty rifles and a machine gun. Also found within the building were various documents giving a complete nominal roll of the ELAS company that were defending the brewery.

Following the success of the assault on the brewery, Gwyn's immediate attention turned to those buildings surrounding him that were filled with deadly snipers. His battalion systematically searched each building from wall to wall, arresting any, and all suspects they encountered. Once a suspect had been identified, they would be sent to the battalion HQ where they would be held in the POW cage. From there, they would be interrogated to determine what degree of association they had, if any, with the communist rebels.

Gwyn entered each building with caution, aware that anyone and anything may lurk behind each door he forced open. The language barrier created the biggest issue as it prevented him from asking direct questions to those that he encountered, but his training allowed him to assess them based on their body language and any items in their possession. The task of differentiating a member of ELAS that was masking their allegiances, from a regular family man who was frightened and traumatised by the war being raged in his community, was difficult. Knowing the extent to which the rebels would go to evade capture, Gwyn thought it best to err on the side of caution and apprehend anyone who fit the profile of an enemy and allow his superiors to determine their allegiance. He understood the ordeal that he was submitting these individuals to, and the guilt played on his mind, but the idea that anyone who slipped through the net may be the next man to fire at him or his comrades left him no choice but to play it safe.

At 1200 hrs. whilst escorting a group of 40 men from the area of buildings they had being searching to the POW cage, a sudden barrage of sniper fire was unleashed upon them. The prisoners, who were unarmed and bound, leapt to cover whilst the men who escorted them attempted to pinpoint the area from which the attack was coming. They narrowed the sniper nest to a small area just outside the perimeter and observed it over the coming hours. One particular sniper continued to cause problems for the British, killing 1 troop and wounding another 9. With the window that housed the sniper identified, British commanders decided to take no chances and dispatched a tank to destroy the nest. Once cleared, the sniper fire eased.

Civilians

It was difficult to recognise who the innocent civilians were, not only because of the way the enemy mingled amongst them but because sometimes the innocent civilians were forced into acts of terror. ELAS often used women or even children, who were far too young to understand the political tug of war that controlled their lives, to pass on messages or lead men into ambushes. Despite being deceived by these 'innocent' civilians, the British men understood the position they found themselves in. They simply needed to do what they could in order to protect themselves and their families, much like Gwyn considered himself to be doing.

The conditions for the residents that were trapped in the ELAS-controlled areas of Athens were appalling. They had next to no water, so the little they did have would have been carefully rationed, and they had no food other than the small scraps they were fed by the rebels for tasks they had carried out or what crumbs the British could spare. They were subject to strict curfews imposed by the British troops and were only permitted to roam freely between Midday and 2 PM. If the area in which they lived had seen no rebel action for 48 hours, the curfew would be relaxed from 10 AM to 2 PM. But as the British steadily cleared sections of Athens, expanding their perimeter day by day, they would liberate the people who were determined to be innocent following an interrogation. A carefully designed plan was drawn up by the British in order to convince the locals to side with them rather than the rebels. They would allocate ration cards and distribute food accordingly, they would provide clothing and ensure the civilians had shelter, convincing them that the British were there to help them, and highlight the rebels for the immoral monsters that they were. Once an area had been incorporated into British control, the curfew would be relaxed further, allowing locals to freely roam between 10 AM and 6 PM.

During the festive period of 1944, the British army arranged a food distribution event for the Greek people. Civilians were invited from all over Athens and would be entertained with anecdotes and casual conversations with the British troops and hierarchy. Interacting with the innocent victims of this war helped in their mission to reassure the people that the British were allies and could be trusted.

A Greek Victory

Soon after the joyous interaction between the civilians and soldiers had come to an end, the new year loomed, and Gwyn was continuing in his work along with his unit by clearing an abandoned school that was apparently occupied by ELAS. This information had been volunteered by a local woman, so the troops were sceptical. With the immoral tactics of the rebels, this may have been an attempt to lead them into an ambush, but the importance of the information meant it must be investigated.

The men entered the building cautiously, not knowing what they would encounter, but it soon became apparent that the building had long since been deserted. They continued to search the building, room by room, with the hope of finding a shred of information that may help their officials back at HQ. Upon entering a large hall, Gwyn was horrified by the sight that met him. Lying in pools of dry blood were lashes that had heavily frayed at the ends. They had obviously been extensively used before being tossed in the blood of those that they had tortured. The evidence that remained in the hall suggested it had been used as a flogging house, which confirmed the rumours of the inhumane acts that these rebels were guilty of. Also found inside the building were two food dumps containing an estimated half-tonne of powdered soup, powdered milk and German tinned food. During a time of vast starvation among the civilians, this food was quickly distributed among them.

Despite the horrific discovery in the hall, the chain of command considered the remains within the school a promising sign. With such an important rebel facility, along with vital food abandoned, the

British believed that this was evidence that the ELAS were retreating at an increasingly swift rate and their numbers and areas in which they operated were shrinking by the day. The intuition showed by the men in charge turned out to be correct, as by the 6th of January 1945, it was officially announced that Athens had been cleared of ELAS fighters.

With the news of success in Greece, Gwyn knew the significance of this victory and its timing. With the situation in Europe looking encouraging, and victory looming increasingly close, this was the first time the prospect of peace had realistically crossed Gwyn's mind. Germany's vast empire looked to be shrinking each day and the onward momentum of the Allies was crushing the Nazi's will to fight. The atmosphere amongst Gwyn and his comrades was one of elation and relief. The hope that they had fought their last battle was at last a genuine possibility. Although Gwyn knew there remained work to do, he hoped that the fierce battles that had consumed his identity were a thing of the past.

Following the end of hostilities in Athens, Gwyn and the 2/4th were moved to Kipseli, in the northeast of Greece, where they continued with light training and the occasional drill. But their time there was often spent enjoying a well-earned rest. They had no operational duties, but Gwyn and most others chose to spend time in the town helping locals clean, repair and reconstruct their lives. The opportunity to work side by side with the Greek people meant a lot to Gwyn, but the joy with which the Greek people celebrated the British was incomparable. They adored them and insisted that they owed them a great deal for the kindness and compassion shown towards the end of the war.

Although the troops provided festive hospitality for the locals in 1944, the task of continuously extending their control of Athens by capturing areas, street by street, prevented them from having the opportunity to celebrate Christmas, so it was delayed for a later date. This long-awaited festive celebration finally materialised on the 3rd of February, only three days after Gwyn was sent to Petromangoula. Each company occupied an outbuilding within the grounds of a cotton factory where they were stationed and were able to celebrate enthusiastically. With the festivities playing second fiddle to the looming victory, the men were overflowing with excitement. Towards the evening of their makeshift Christmas, a crowd of officials from the village travelled the short distance to the cotton factory to thank the 2/4th

Battalion for all that they had done for the village, and Greece. The friendly visit ended with the presentation of a Lamb that was gifted to Colonel Mitchel, who commanded the 2/4th, as a gesture of appreciation. A huge honour in their culture, especially during a time of starvation and hardship.

Gwyn's time in Petromangoula however, was not entirely spent celebrating. The end of the German occupation and the defeat of the ELAS forces left Greece completely unable to support itself. The situation left behind by the Nazis and the communists meant that any political or authoritative power once held by the Greeks had been relinquished. Once liberated, the country was handed a clean slate to rebuild its civilisation. Government officials were elected and appointed as were the positions of authority that came with them, such as the heads of education, health, and police. This, however, took time. For the elected party to create an infrastructure of leadership within each department, and then for that leadership to rebuild and reorganise, was a large undertaking. This is where the British army was at hand to support them. For that reason, Gwyn and his 2/4th were sent to Petromangoula. They were ordered to police the village until adequate organisation was restored within the Greek police force. Although sometimes a challenging assignment, the responsibility of overseeing the village's law enforcement was largely breaking up petty squabbles and resolving issues impartially. Within a month, progress had been made in the Greek structure of authority and the 2/4th were able to move back to Kipseli and then on to Khalikis, where their regular routine of punishing training would resume. Their bodies had been finely tuned by theatres of war under the most extreme circumstances, but readjusting to a training regime after any form of respite was a gruelling task, especially with the rumours and reports that soon the war would be won. The psychological edge that war and its desperation created was difficult to maintain even during hostilities, but with the complacency of peace creeping in, the killer instinct that had been drilled into them began to fall dormant.

CHAPTER SEVENTEEN

Crete

With the unconditional surrender of Nazi Germany looming, the anticipation of victory was palpable. Gwyn spent his time dreaming of sailing toward the white cliffs of Dover with his two good friends by his side, the seagulls squawking overhead as the cheering crowd waves from the harbour. He smiled warmly at the thought of touching British soil and sucking in the fresh Welsh air. He longed for his home at Min-Yr-Afon and his family within, who he imagined to be sitting around the fire listening to the wireless that spoke of the progress in Europe.

His dream inched closer with each day until the 6th of May when he was told that their commanding officer, Colonel Mitchell was to address the men with his latest orders. With excitement in the air,

Gwyn stood and awaited the news, convinced it would be of his departure from foreign soil. As Colonel Mitchell began to speak, it became clear by his body language and tone of voice that this would not be the long-awaited departure speech the men had anticipated. He brought orders for a new objective. This time, in Crete.

The battle of Crete and the German occupation that followed, caused the same damage to the island as it did on the mainland of Greece. The starvation and devastation were rife, and the attitude amongst the Cretans was as negative as anywhere in the world. The community were bound together by the culture and communal relationships you could only find on a small island, making it even more difficult to endure the harrowing pain and suffering caused to loved ones and people who belong to their community. Men were imprisoned or forced to work for the Nazi war efforts as their wives, girlfriends and mothers watched on helplessly. The true devastation caused to families would take generations to heal, some never did.

Defending the Nazis

Gwyn stood on the deck of an elegant destroyer

that moved effortlessly across the water. He watched the waves crash over the Cretan shores as they approached Souda Bay at the north of Crete, near the city of Chania. He disembarked on the 8th of May 1945 just as the sun began to warm towards its summer peak. The clear blue sky's reflection glistened on the surface of the bay. The beauty of the coastline continued to impress as Gwyn ventured ashore. The harbour seemed calmer and more peaceful than the ones he had previously experienced. British troops still occupied the bay, but the reduced numbers and urgency at which they moved created a jovial atmosphere of peace.

Though all seemed relaxed, the situation in Crete had been complex. In October of 1944, the British and Germans signed a unique and peculiar treaty which allowed the Germans to withdraw peacefully and gradually from Crete whilst being left undisturbed, and in return, the Germans would give up Athens. Both sides kept to their agreement and Athens was vacated. Though Greece had been liberated, Crete remained under German occupation with around 17,000 troops remaining. So, for the 7 months from October 44 until the unconditional surrender of Germany in May 45, Crete was ruled by a strange Anglo-German command.

During this period, the British were waiting on the outcome of the Greek civil war, with their plan B to declare Crete an independent state should their attempts to overcome the rebels fail. Once the rebels were ejected from Athens and a German surrender looked likely, the British began to move troops into Crete. Eventually, May 1945 saw the surrender of Germany and with it, Crete. The German troops that maintained a strange rule over the island had now become British POWs.

The mission that faced Gwyn on this beautiful island was to take over the control of an area containing German POWs and to escort them to Souda Bay where he would oversee their departure. The expectations of Gwyn and his fellow soldiers for the task at hand was that they would spend a few weeks standing guard as the now harmless Germans waited to be taken away to an unknown fate. The reality of the task however was more difficult and complex than he had imagined. Though the Germans had surrendered, not just politically but also mentally, and offered no resistance, there were other threats for Gwyn to be wary of.

The Cretan people ferociously resisted the German

occupation, and although they were glad to see it come to an end, there remained an untainted hatred for the Germans. That was the sentiment shared amongst the civilians throughout Greece, but where Crete differed from the mainland was in their animosity towards the British.

Gwyn left Greece under a cloud of heroism and celebration, which was welcomed by the men after years of hostility and hatred being aimed at them. Gwyn assumed the gratitude shown toward them by the locals would be shared throughout the Greek islands, but on arrival at Souda Bay, there seemed a thick cloud of animosity that hovered over the Cretian people which was directed towards the British as well as the German prisoners.

The strained relationship between the troops and the civilians stemmed from the agreement made between the British and Germans. While the Nazis were driven out of mainland Greece and other nations of Europe, the deal saw Nazi rule continue, although under reduced authority, in Crete. The Cretans felt, understandably, let down and abandoned by the British. So, their underlying issues existed before Gwyn's arrival, but with the Germans having now surrendered, a hotbed of tension was created.

The Cretan civilians saw the collapse of Nazi Germany as their opportunity to obtain a grain of revenge on the men left behind on their island. They had the bitter taste of war left in their mouths and were determined to feed their hunger for German blood. Due to the potential civilian onslaught on the area that contained the Germans, the British were required to stand guard around the clock. This left Gwyn in the unusual position of having to defend the prisoners from the public, rather than the public from the prisoners.

Already displaying their displeasure with the British troops, the Cretan public's irritations grew further as they were prevented access to Germans by the men standing guard. They couldn't comprehend how the men who once fought tirelessly to kill the Allied troops were now being defended by them. Their trust for the British had diminished and this issue had not helped to restore it. Gwyn and his comrades attempted to disarm the tension with kindness and gestures of goodwill, which were well received in the local vicinity and made the local people feel far more comfortable in the British presence but did little to ease the island's sorrow.

Souda Bay

Souda Bay is a natural harbour that sits around 15km long and about 2km wide, making it an easily defendable port. It was used during the evacuation of Allied troops during the battle of Crete in 1941 and was therefore well defended once the Germans had gained control. As the German defences were stationed around the bay at the time of surrender, it became the main area in which they were detained and the main port from which they would be deported.

Heavily manned British ships would dock in the bay regularly between May and August 1945, each one was loaded with Germans who were increasingly concerned for their future. The ships would be cramped and uncomfortable, and their destination remained unknown.

When the news of a ship's imminent arrival came through to Gwyn's superiors, he would be ordered to round up the next portion of prisoners that were to embark. They would be quickly ushered out of the prison and into awaiting TCVs. Once several vehicles were packed with men, they would head off to Souda Bay with heavily armed British troops both leading and trailing the convoy. The heavily guarded convoy acted as a deterrent for any potential escapes, or more likely, attacks from local vigilantes.

As Gwyn watched the men board these colossal ships, he couldn't help but wonder what conditions they would face onboard. His journey from Clyde to Algeria was as difficult a journey as he had ever faced, and that was close to luxurious when compared to what these prisoners were to face. They remained bound together, each leading the man behind further into the bowels of the ship. Once the ship contained a number of prisoners that far exceeded the maximum capacity, it would slowly edge away from the dock and disappear into the distance.

The destination that awaited the ship remained a mystery to Gwyn. The fate of POWs was a controversial topic amongst the men, as some insisted they should now be released following the surrender of the Nazis. Others held opposing opinions and insisted that they should be sentenced to death. However, in reality, they would likely be made to provide labour for the rebuilding of the Allied nations that had suffered at the hands of their leaders and comrades.

Mission Accomplished

With the island of Crete clear of German POWs, on the 28th of July, 1945 orders for Gwyn to return to mainland Greece were given. He reversed the route that brought him to Crete 3 months earlier and went ashore at Piraeus. From there, he travelled directly to Yannina, where he settled for 2 months. Despite having no military operational role, the troops were encouraged to use their time to assist and reassure the community. They rebuilt homes and roads as well as supported groups of farmers and businesses as they reintegrated within the community. Alongside their work to support the civilians, they also provided their services to the Greek national guard and police that continued to struggle with conflict with the communists along the Albanian border. Cautious not to be drawn into further warfare, Gwyn and his 2/4th would encourage peace and help to restore order when troubles would arise.

Gwyn's final posting of his time in Greece would come on the 22nd of October when the 2/4th were sent south to Patras. The beautiful city of Patras sits at the foot of Mount Panachaikon, overlooking the Gulf of Patras. The area was an awe-inspiring spectacle, the rich colours that autumn brought with it produced a spectrum of beauty.

Gwyn's war concluded here at Patras where he whiled away the hours relaxing. They had no operational role at Patras, and they occupied a pleasant estate about a mile north of town and only a hundred yards from the sea. Their sun-soaked bodies rested and healed from years of abuse and neglect. Their rested minds began the process of healing wounds that haunted their thoughts.

CHAPTER EIGHTEEN

Back to Blighty

With Gwyn's days filled with rest coming to an end, his thoughts again turned to home, as they often did, but with fellow soldiers slowly being released, the fantasy that was for so long out of reach looked to be becoming a reality that he sensed looming. As autumn turned to winter, more colleagues and friends left and the area around the estate grew quieter. Men received their summons to British soil and eagerly counted down the days before their departure. They would say their goodbyes and swap contact information with those they had bonded with. Gwyn watched on with hope that it would soon be him.

As 1945 came to an end, the troops that remained in Greece entered 1946 wishing for a peaceful year of happiness with their loved ones. The festive time of year always caused homesickness, and thoughts of their family always played on the men's minds, but never more than the new year of 1946. With the war over, and the herd thinning out, they knew they were tantalisingly close to home.

At the beginning of January, Gwyn finally had the news he had been waiting for. He was being sent back to Britain where he would be released from service. His discharge paperwork was complete, and he was issued with his documents of release. His military conduct was described as 'exemplary'. The comments made by his commanding officer were as follows:

"A clean, honest and industrious soldier. He is a good hardworking man on whom reliance can always be placed. Of exemplary character, he has given loyal service to the battalion since joining. Previously been employed as a gunner in a Heavy AA and saw service in CMF. He has given extremely useful service to his company in and outside his ordinary course of duty. Returning to his old job, I am certain he will give to it the same loyalty that he

has given the army in the past. A man I can thoroughly recommend."

The 15th of January 1946 saw Gwyn finally set foot on British soil once more. It was the moment he had spent the last 3 years fantasising about. Each time he closed his eyes for a moment's rest, he saw the distant glow of the white cliffs of Dover approaching, but experiencing this surreal feeling felt almost too much. The overwhelming joy and sense of belonging he felt as he breathed the fresh British air brought tears to his eyes.

On the 17th of January, his paperwork had been completed and he had officially been released from the army and into a nation that was wrestling between the monumental task of rebuilding structures and lives and celebrating the end of a conflict that had been bitterly felt by all. The mix of emotions that blew through the air made it difficult to adjust to life in a Peaceful Britain as the nation began to piece together its new reality.

Gwyn wasted no time in finding his way home. The familiar landscape of Britain began to become increasingly sparse and rural as he travelled west into his beloved Pembrokeshire. The gradual slopes grew into rolling hills as the towering peaks of the Preseli mountains rose on the horizon. The familiar cobblestoned streets and thatched roofs came into view and Gwyn's heart filled with warmth as he had finally made it home to Letterston. The village remained untouched by the horrors of war, but somehow Letterston felt different. The village pub that once housed the thirsty men who congregated to share stories now seemed smaller. The hustle of the streets that lined the village now seemed quieter. Gwyn considered that the village, which remained the picturesque slice of countryside, perhaps hadn't changed at all, and the change may lay within himself.

Gwyn reached Min-Yr-Afon and was greeted by the warm embrace of his loving family. Martha, Lewis, Glyn, Vincent, and Keith all stood in the doorway with beaming smiles. Gwyn greeted them all individually with a warm embrace. The years of adventure and love that preceded the war came flooding back.

Despite the ever-present love and connection that Gwyn felt for his family, something had changed. He knew something within him had changed. He had left an innocent boy who relied upon his family for stability, wisdom, strength, and love. But seven years of brutal warfare had matured him into a steely, reserved man with a protective shell that made emotion difficult. Seven years of portraying a hard-faced warrior with no fear or remorse was difficult to ignore. Showing emotion could get you killed on the battlefield, so Gwyn's ruthless mentality of hiding emotions became a habit that eventually moulded the man who returned to Min-Yr-Afon.

A New Normal

Adjusting to post-war Britain was difficult enough for civilians and troops, but the slow pace of life that made Letterston the tranquil escape made the adjustment difficult for Gwyn. He had grown accustomed to the military life of planning, routine and precision, where every second of each day was tightly regulated and allowed little flexibility. Life in Letterston stood in stark contrast to what he had come to know, with time emerging as his new enemy. Each morning brought with it a day promising nothing but endless monotony.

Gwyn tried to satisfy his restless need to be productive by hard work. He continuously searched for his next mission. He toiled on farms and helped local builders to fill his days, with his evenings spent socialising amongst those who continued to celebrate their returning sense of normality.

He wrestled with his attempts to adapt and tame the soldier's mentality that had kept him alive. Whilst externally appearing to be successful, the silent struggle continued to rage within him. His tough exterior, unwilling to show weakness, hindered his recovery as his friends and family remained ignorant of his need for support.

Continuing to survive was the only thing he knew, so Gwyn forged ahead with his unrelenting desire to fill his days with work and socialising. He mixed with friends, both old and new, around the village, bonding with those who shared in his experiences of war. The opportunities to converse with fellow veterans were a welcome distraction for Gwyn, as the vast majority of the population of Letterston had never left the village, so their understanding of his experiences was basic.

As time moved on, Gwyn began to struggle with the conversations of war that once distracted him from the daily monotony. The memories of horror that the veterans and their stories brought with them become too much. Gwyn did all he could to forget the turmoil he had both witnessed and caused. Contributing to one of the world's most devastating conflicts in history, was a scar that became too painful to bear.

A Second Chance at Life

The pain and suffering that continued to burn in Gwyn's every thought failed to subside, and he continued with the brave face that he forced onto the surface. He maintained his resistance to share his troubles, which only worsened. His mind became congested with thoughts of terror with no method of release.

His hard work and social life continued to mask his issues, whilst also allowing opportunities to create new connections and relationships. Soon after returning home, he met a young woman named Mary-Ann Harries, who lived at a small holding between the small villages of Castle Morris and Mathry, that were nearby.

Meeting Mary had as much of an impact on Gwyn's life as that letter that had arrived through the post in 1939. In Mary, Gwyn found himself a soulmate. The minute they met; Gwyn's troubles began to subside. Mary represented a future for him that was far removed from the past that haunted him. She acted as both a distraction and motivation to move forward.

The ability to show his feelings towards someone remained difficult for Gwyn due to his experiences at war, as building relationships with men only for them to be tragically ended, was difficult to leave behind. The continuous heartache that lingered within him created a protective layer that defended his emotions. But once Gwyn and Mary began their courtship, he quickly felt the heartache melt away. His mind opened to the idea of love and a future without the conflict and loss he knew so well.

The January of 1947 marked a turning point in Gwyn's life, a point in which he could leave his past behind and begin a new life as he and Mary married. The nuptials combined two families that would be linked together forever. Gwyn's appearance of an outgoing, confident man had merely been a façade for so long, but with Mary having seven siblings, the size of his extended family alone gave him the lift he needed to begin the retrieval of his true personality.

With Gwyn now having a beloved wife with whom he could finally feel comfortable enough to share his feelings, his mind began to clear of the tragedies that once cluttered it. He and Mary began a life together that would become his redemption, but it did not come without more hardship.

A Month of Loss

Confident that his darkest days were behind him and with the memories of war seemingly ebbing from his memory, April 1948 had a profound impact on both Gwyn and Mary. The events of that month would impact them both as individuals but would galvanize them as a pair, reinforcing the relationship and bonds that tied them together.

Mary-Ann's early life revolved around family. She, her 4 sisters and 3 brothers grew up with a close bond that was instilled in them by their parents. Their father Gwynne, and mother, also Mary, worked hard to provide for their large family despite the hardships of the era. Mary-Ann was a woman of morals and integrity that were instilled in her by her father. But with the strength and independence these characteristics produced also came the stubborn nature that was embedded in his DNA. Neither strong-willed mind could ever be changed.

The love that Mary exuded was a testament to her mother's kind, caring nature. The love she felt for her children shaped each one of their personalities, but none more than Mary-Ann's. She inherited the warmth that her mother portrayed to her, which in turn, she passed on to her children.

This devotion that Mary showed her children made April of 1948 one of the most difficult times of Mary-Ann's life. Her mother, Mary, passed away from cancer at the age of 56. The ripples of grief were felt through the extended family including her son-in-law, Gwyn. He, much like everyone who knew Mary, felt her loss, but the pain he felt for his wife added to his sorrow.

Such a loss, and the suffering that comes with it, create a bond between those who share in the grief, and this was true of Gwyn and Mary-Ann. Gwyn supported his wife in mourning with gentle comfort. He stood by her side in her time of need, and it was his strength that sustained her. However, the strength that they possessed was tested further when more tragic news struck the couple.

Word reached Gwyn that his father, David, needed to see him. Only a short walk to David's house, Gwyn curiously visited him. The sombre atmosphere in the room highlighted the seriousness of the conversation that was to be had. David, sitting behind a table with a familiar look of anguish painted on his face, pointed down to a folded piece of paper that lay in front of him. Gwyn leant over while picking up the document and unfolding it, his concern grew. He glanced over the letter quickly, without needing to read line by line, he had grasped the distressing message.

Gwyn's brother, Owen Morgan had passed away whilst serving in the merchant navy. The details that the letter held were vague and the lack of information created frustration and curiosity to add to the grief that Gwyn already felt. In the coming days, more details filtered through to the family, and the reason for the ambiguous letter became clearer.

Owen was serving aboard the MV Atlantic City in Fremantle, Western Australia at the time of the tragedy. After the full details had emerged it was revealed that Owen had been working on a staging that hung over the side of the vessel. He was painting the ship with two shipmates, one of which was Seaman John Donovan whose official statement read as follows,

"Morgan's foot suddenly slipped into the space between the stage and the ship's side and he fell through the gap into the water.

I jumped in with my clothes on and grabbed Morgan who seemed to be floating motionless just under the surface.
I think he might have hit his head against the side of the ship. I finally had to let him go. "

Owen's body was lost as it sunk into the depths. Despite days of dredging the harbour, the authorities were still unable to find his body until eventually, it floated up onto the surface days later. The incident occurred on Wednesday the 7th of April 1948, but it wasn't until Sunday the 11th that the body was recovered. However, the MV Atlantic City had sailed on Saturday the 10th, leaving nobody that was able to identify the body. Fortunately, the coroner was in possession of Owen's British seaman's identity card, which held his fingerprints, and therefore was able to identify him. He was buried on April the 14th 1948 in Fremantle cemetery in a grave that remains unmarked and unvisited by any family members.

The news evoked cherished memories of his brother as Gwyn considered the irony of the incident. Owen had spent years navigating the perilous oceans filled with formidable enemy ships and U-boats, only for his life to be cut painfully short by a task as mundane as painting.

The years of loss that Gwyn had experienced were beginning to subside, but the loss of his mother-in-law and his brother within days of each other undoubtedly caused a setback. With the married couple mourning both their losses and the sorrow, they felt for each other, the strength that they conjured up for each other was the driving force that bound them together for a lifetime of love and happiness. It was this that created a footing upon which they built their lives together.

On to Happier Times

Despite the early hardship in their relationship, Gwyn and Mary continued to support each other through their grief with their future shaping a route from the anguish. With family creating the foundations of Mary's personality, and the absence of family that Gwyn had experienced, it was important for them to build a family of their own.

Their marriage grew from strength to strength with the arrival of their first child, Gwyneth. Amongst the shadows within Gwyn's mind, lay a warm and loving father. Although firm and somewhat distant at times, there was always an underlying love for his family that he showed not with words, but with his everyday actions. Displaying his love and pride proved difficult as the battle he faced with the darkness remained at the back of his mind. Despite his difficulties, he provided a loving home for his new daughter and was delighted when he and Mary soon brought further love into their household.

More children soon warmed the home that he and Mary had created in Min-Y-Llan, Letterston, with Shirley, Gareth and Perry completing their family. Although Gwyn remained reserved in vocalising the pride he felt for his family, he silently relied upon his children to continually make him a better person. The unconditional love that was weaved through the fabric of the family opened his mind and heart to the possibility that this happiness he felt warm his soul, may last forever. Deep within his thoughts, he began to consider that this cocoon of joy that he had found, may not result in heartbreak and loss. This may be different to the family members and brothers of war that were taken from him. The idea of being content and consistently feeling love filled him with joy, but the rugged mentality that carried him through the deadly battles of war prevented him from sharing his joy, and instead, he continued to air his discomfort with annoyances as mundane as one of the children changing the television over from the BBC. His irritation would often be vocalized with disapproving tutting, muttered under his breath.

The burden of Gwyn's relentless need to keep his mind occupied eased when he found employment at the Royal Naval Armament Depot (RNAD) at Trecwn, only 3 miles from his home. He was employed as a Storeman which consisted of physical labour that continued to challenge his robust body. The organisation of a Royal Navy depot fitted with Gwyn's personality as the rigorous planning and development was the nearest thing to that of the conditions that he had thrived under at war. He continued to work tirelessly at RNAD Trecwn throughout his working life, and after 25 years of loyal service, Gwyn was awarded the Imperial Service Medal, which he proudly received with his wife at his side.

With a content family and professional life, Gwyn had overcome the horrors of war and the demons that followed it. His persistent need to endure each challenge that faced him carved a resilient man with a warm and loving heart. From a motherless boy to a warrior who defied the incredible odds that were stacked against him, the spirit that lay within Gwyn was nothing short of heroic, but the heroism of war was merely a grain of sand on the beach of his life. It was the mental fortitude that he displayed to overcome the hardships that silently plagued him, whilst continuing to forge a path forward to find inner peace and happiness, that is truly heroic. It was his remarkable resolve in the face of hardship that should be considered inspiring. His family, and the immense strength that he was able to conjure up to build it, is the legacy that he leaves behind today. And it is that that should always be remembered.

GWYN – THE LIFE OF AN UNSUNG SOLDIER

Printed in Great Britain
by Amazon